THE CHURCH, THE MINISTRY,

AND REUNION

THE CHURCH,

THE MINISTRY,

AND REUNION

BY W. NORMAN PITTENGER

GREENWICH/CONNECTICUT/1957

© 1957 by The Seabury Press, Incorporated

Library of Congress Catalog Card Number: 57-5797

Design by Stefan Salter

Printed in the United States of America

FOR

LAWRENCE ROSE,

DEAN OF THE GENERAL SEMINARY,

AS A TOKEN OF CONTINUING

ESTEEM AND AFFECTION

PREFACE

THE General Convention of 1955, meeting at Honolulu, directed that the Episcopal Church should study, during the three years until the next convention, the reunion of Christian communions in the Church of South India. This book is a small contribution to that study; it is printed in the hope that something may be said in it which will have value for clergy and lay-people who are following the directive of our highest governing body.

It will be apparent to the reader, before he finishes these pages, that my sympathies are with the South India Church —and that I should wish that our own church may follow the action of our sister-communion in England and accord such recognition to it as may be possible in terms of our own canons and traditions. But the main object of this book is not to argue for the Church of South India, but to get at something much more basic than any particular plan or proposal—namely, the root question of the nature of the ministry in relation to the Church of God which is the Body of the Living Christ. It must be in terms of such basic theological considerations that any reunion of Christendom takes place.

I believe that the best way in which we can follow the directive of Honolulu is by such a study; then it will be apparent, in my judgment, that a plan such as that of South India is indeed a step towards the eventual visible unity of the whole Body of Christ in its fullness.

W. Norman Pittenger

CONTENTS

· ix ·

THE CHURCH, THE MINISTRY,

AND REUNION

I

SOME PRELIMINARIES ON THE CHURCH

AND MINISTRY

IT HAS often been remarked, in the discussion of the problems faced by the Christian Church as we struggle towards a reunited Christendom, that one point of difference appears to be insurmountable: the meaning of the Christian ministry. It is increasingly recognized that the stumbling block which remains after other obstacles have been cleared away is the deep disagreement about the nature and function of the minister in Christ's Church. Agreement about many, if not all, the articles of the faith seems possible. A common mind on the principles of Christian morality is not too hard to achieve, once initial prejudices and presuppositions have been examined. Even in respect to Christian worship, many think that general statements may be made which can find wide if not universal acceptance. But as to the ministry—here, indeed, we are faced with a difficulty that seems to be as real today as it was when reunion discussions began a half-century ago.

The difficulty is not necessarily one which divides each denomination or tradition from every other. There are, indeed, quite extensive areas of agreement among many Christians concerning the ministry of the Church. The problem first arises between two general groups of Christian communions: between those who subscribe to what we may call an "incidental" view of the ministry, and those who maintain a "necessary" view. And there is a further difference among those who hold to the latter, or "necessary," view. This time it is between the group who believe that in the ministry which is necessary to the Church, a certain kind of functioning is both implicit in and necessary to it if it is indeed to be essential; and the group who believe in a necessary ministry but are prepared to allow for considerable variation in the understanding of the ministerial office so far as its functioning is concerned.

Under whatever terms the discussion may be conducted, these two sets of differences are the real meaning of the disagreement between what may be called the "Catholic," and what may be called the "Protestant," sides in the reunion problem.

Differences of View

The differences are rooted in differing conceptions of the nature of the Church's tradition, and seem to persist even when some mutual understanding, if not agreement, may be reached through a careful restatement of theological ideas. It is fundamental to the Catholic position, however conceived, to insist that *order* is closely related to the *faith* of the Church. It is not a secondary, still less an irrelevant, matter. Protestant thought, even in circles which take what might well be described as a relatively "high" view of the ministry, generally tends to consider the whole question of order as in a quite different class from faith; sometimes it is placed very definitely as a secondary matter, far below those concerns of faith and life which alone should be given primary importance.

Yet it is the opinion of the writer of these pages that to a large degree the disagreement on the nature and function of the ministry is due also to semantic difficulties. Indeed, one might say that the problem of the meaning of words is much more serious in Christian theology than has usually been recognized. When we get at the *real* meaning of the words we use, rather than rest content with some superficial meaning, we often find that we are really saying the same thing as are our separated Christian brethren who happen to use different words. The *words* have called up alien or objectionable ideas; and these have foreclosed any understanding between us. One of the purposes of the present study is to probe beneath the *words* to the real *meaning*. In this way, it may be possible to reach a better understanding and perhaps even resolve some of the differences.

The Relation of the Ministry to the Church

But in discussions of the meaning of the ministry there is another and deeper concern. This is the relation of the ministry to the nature and the significance of the Church. All too often, the study of the ministry has been undertaken without adequate consideration of the Church for and in which the ministry carries on its work. The result has been the establishment of a whole series of ideas, some of them false and many of them pernicious, which not only make any mutual understanding an impossibility but also lead to erroneous conceptions of the nature of the Christian ministry itself. For this reason our first task is to study the nature and function of the Church of Christ, and to consider the ministry in relation to that nature and function; unless we do this, our whole enterprise is fruitless.

This approach is made necessary by two quite opposite and, in our view, erroneous positions about the nature and function of the ministry that have appeared in recent writing on the subject. One of these positions states that somehow the clergy "make" the Church.[1] The other position affirms that priesthood must be grounded first and essentially in the being of the Body of Christ itself, but the position does not recognize with equal clarity that this affirmation can really have no permanent significance for men living historical lives, unless this priesthood is visibly and externally expressed and made manifest.[2]

It is the aim of this chapter to discuss these ways—both mistaken, in our opinion—of conceiving the ministry in relation to the Church. But first of all we must be clear as to the meaning of the Church itself. Fortunately in our time there has been a marked recovery of the New Testament and the early Christian understanding of the Church's reality. Not only among those who might be thought to stand by tradition for a "high" conception of the Church, but also among theologians of more Protestant background, the Church today is commonly agreed to be an essential element in the Gospel, because it is "the Spouse and Bride of Christ."

An excellent illustration of this agreed position may be seen in Dr. William Robinson's recent work, *The Biblical Doctrine of the Church*. The author, who is an English member of the denomination known as the Disciples of Christ, maintains that "in reality, the Church is Christ manifest in the flesh, as Jesus of Nazareth was God manifest in the flesh" (p. 101). Dr. Robinson uses phrases which have often been thought to be distinctively Catholic, when he writes that "the Church is the perpetuation of the Incarnation," and like its Lord "is both human and divine" (p. 103). And we learn from this writer that on the basis of New Testament teaching, there can be no possibility of speaking of "Christianity without the Church" (p. 189).

Dr. Robinson's position may be taken as typical of many Protestant theologians of our day, once they are confronted with the actual New Testament picture of the meaning of the Church and the significance of membership in it. Such scholars as Dr. C. Harold Dodd, in England, and Dr. John Knox, in America, are agreed in the defense of this view.[3]

An equally important and interesting development has occurred in circles traditionally "Catholic." Here the somewhat mechanical and legalistic idea of the Church, which has often marked popular Roman and some Anglican "tractarian" writing, has been modified by the influence of the "liturgical movement," with its strong grasp of the idea of the Church as a vital organism. Theologians of the

Roman communion, like Mersch in France, and Adam in Germany, can be taken as typical of this change.[4] In the Anglican Communion, A. G. Hebert's *The Form of the Church* is an excellent example of the new spirit in Catholic thought. The Church for Hebert is "a living body," even while it has a definite "form"; its very existence "presupposes the presence in it of the Spirit of God to animate it with life and make it a living fellowship of men bound together by love." The Church is to be understood as being what Scripture declares it to be: "the Bride, the Body, the Flock, the Temple, the City . . . the sphere of the Divine Reign." [5]

Traditionally, Eastern Orthodox thought has also maintained a vitalistic doctrine of the Church in strong opposition to what it has regarded as the "dead" and legalistic view of the West.[6]

The Meaning of the Church

It is now plain that the Holy Catholic Church can no longer be seen as an adventitious "gathering" of believing Christians, on the one hand; nor on the other hand, can it be viewed as if it were a machine set in operation by the Founder of Christianity. It is "the mystical Body of Christ, which is the blessed company of all faithful people"—that is, of all people who are possessed by the given faith, and know and share this faith within a fellowship whose reality is the indwelling life of Christ Himself through the Holy Spirit.

The Church is a unity, in that it is related to the one

Christ and finds unity in Him, as His Body. It is holy, since it is called and set apart from the rest of the world for the explicit purpose of mediating the life of God in Christ through the Spirit, thereby bringing forth the fruits of the Spirit in the lives of its members. It is catholic, not only in that its mission and message are for all men, at all times, in all places, but, more profoundly, in that it is constituted *kath 'olou*, hence "catholic"—which in its Greek derivation means "in terms of wholeness." And the Church is apostolic, because it is based upon the historical actuality to which the apostolic record bears witness; and it is, therefore, both dependent upon, and the continuation of, the apostolic community with its faith, its worship, its life in grace, and (as we shall show in a later chapter) its "ministerial" expression.

This is the Church as it has manifested its nature and performed its functions, first in New Testament times, then in the early days of its history as we may recover the story from the literature of the period. No other understanding of the Church historically can claim such testimony to its truth; no other view in the present day has that continuity and that identity which guarantee that *here,* whatever may be said of other places of God's revelation, the benefits of the saving work of God in Christ are imparted to sinful men and they are made "members of Christ, the children of God, and inheritors of the kingdom of heaven."

Now if this conception of the Church as the Body of Christ is taken at its full value, it is apparent that any ministerial expression of that Body must find its significance in that it functions *in* and *for* the Body, as well as *to the members* of the Body. We must not, of course, press the analogy of a biological organism to absurd extremes, but we can insist that the metaphor of the body be taken very seriously—much more seriously than Dr. F. W. Dillistone seemed to think desirable in his pamphlet *The Word of God and the People of God.*[7]

The Church as Christ's Body

At any rate, we must carefully note that St. Paul, in I Corinthians and in Colossians, as well as in Romans, seems prepared to go to rather considerable lengths in using the metaphor of "body" for the Church; while Ephesians (which is Pauline in spirit, if not in authorship) is as emphatic on the point as are the views expressed in the undisputed writings of the Apostle. A "biblical theology" of the Church, such as Dr. Dillistone wished to develop, must take seriously this New Testament witness. It is certain that a careful reading of the passages in St. Paul, not to mention the associated ideas in the Johannine literature (there stated in terms of "vine" and "branches"), would suggest that every aspect of the Church's life and work is to be seen as related to Christ in a fashion analogous to that of integral parts to an organic whole. The Church is a divine organism, although doubtless St. Paul did not carry this idea to any "extreme" biological limit.

The Church as Christ's Body, indwelt by the Holy Spirit, who through it and in it makes possible the response of its members to the inner reality of the life of

Christ which is its essential nature, must be seen as the inescapable *prius* for the Christian faith, for the worship of God proper to Christians, and for the life which is peculiar to those who are "in Christ." It must also be seen as the *prius* for the ministry, since the ministry appertains to Christ Himself, Lord of the Church. It is the ministry of His Body through the Holy Spirit.

We must bear these considerations in mind when we turn to the two errors which, as we have said, are frequently found in contemporary discussions of the ministry in its relationship to the Church. The first of these mistaken ideas, we noted, is the view that the ministry is to be given a place which is prior to the Church itself; it is even suggested that it is the apostolic ministry which "makes" the Church, or at least which gives to the Church its peculiarly apostolic character.

The Ministry in New Testament Perspective

Now it is apparent that in the New Testament some evidence may be found which can be read in this way. It is possible to take the story and see in it an account of the creation of the Christian community following after the "call" to the Twelve and the establishment of an embryonic sort of ministry acting for Christ. But this would be a very special kind of reading; it would indeed seem to rest upon an imperfect understanding of the evidence which we possess. For the fact is that so soon as the Lord Jesus had drawn to Him those who heard His preaching, were attracted to His message, and desired to company with Him, the recreation of the old Israel had occurred. Even if not explicitly, yet surely implicitly, the "little flock" (which was not confined to the Twelve) to which Jesus promised that the Father would give the kingdom was the new Israel after the Spirit. It certainly required the events of our Lord's passion, death, resurrection, and ascension to make this flock a self-conscious community in the fullest sense, but the sheer fact of its existence from the earliest days of the ministry of Christ is obvious to any reader of the Synoptic Gospels.

Furthermore, while it is indeed necessary to *distinguish* between the Twelve and the "little flock," it is very misleading to hold to any *discontinuity* in an absolute sense. The Twelve had their function both within and for the "little flock"; they were called to proclaim the saving gospel of the kingdom of God, and presently they were to bear their witness to the saving gospel of the incarnate, crucified, and risen Messiah. But they were not separated in any complete way from the rest of those who followed Jesus in less specialized ways. Similarly, as we read the rest of the New Testament, we can see that while the "apostles" were regarded as possessed of what in more modern language we might call a separate function, and thus did exercise a distinctive ministry in the life of the primitive Christian community, they were not regarded as being discontinuous with the Church itself. They acted for Christ, certainly; but they received their gospel and carried on their work for Christ within the context of the life of the Church whose Lord He was. There was no thought in New Testament times of a relationship to Christ which was not held within and even mediated by the Church, since the Church was Christ's Body within which various members were given particular functions.

If the modern method of New Testament study known as form-criticism has made anything clear, it is surely this fact. The New Testament emerged from, and was addressed to, the community of believers in Christ; it was written "from faith to faith." The inescapable context for any and every remark made in the New Testament about the ministry of the Church, as indeed about everything else in the Christian "way," is precisely this continuing life of the community. Admonitions, exhortations, and explanations are given with the intention of explicating and defining the functions which appertain to those who minister in and for, as well as to, the living Body of the risen Lord. The Church is the Spirit-filled fellowship in which the work of the Lord, once present on earth in fleshly form and now risen from the dead but still present with His people, is known and experienced. The task of the Church is to make His work and His presence more widely known and more universally experienced. The function of the ministry, on any reading of the evidence, is to carry on this task for the Church—that is to say, for the Lord Jesus Christ, risen and triumphant, present in His Church and at work through it by the Holy Spirit. To attempt to separate these several ideas, as we find them in the New Testament, is to put asunder what God has joined together. In the New Testament there is no trace whatsoever of a ministry separate from, or even theoretically conceived as existing apart from, the divine community for which Christ died and in which He still lives as reigning Lord.

The Ontological Status of the Ministry

The opposite error to the one which we have just now criticized is that view which would fail to give genuine ontological status to the ministry. Those who fall into this error have one thing at least to their credit. They are anxious to make it plain that the ministry is always functional to Christ's Church—or, to put it in other words which mean the same thing, to Christ-in-His-Church. In stressing this point, however, they tend to underestimate the persistent and fundamental necessity for structural form in the Body of Christ. If this necessity still seems to some to be too "biological," the critic must make the most of it! It is really implicit in the whole New Testament witness.

The ministry, as such writers sometimes present it, seems to have a certain "accidental" quality in relation to the profound ontological reality which they rightly see in the Church itself. This is due to their failure to recognize that the Christian community is by its very nature immersed in the "timed and spaced" world of our finite human experience. When this is forgotten, no proper accommodation is made to the fact that historical *belonging* implies historical *realities*. But it is exactly in the ministry, as a perennial function of the Body of Christ, that that Body finds a means, on the historical level, for symbolizing its identity through all the inevitable stages of growth and development involved in historical existence. And although the New Testament writers were for the most part certain of a speedy end to the present world, they seem also to have been quite aware of the need for such functioning as would enable the Christian community, in the days before "the end," to carry on its work for the Lord. The principle of ministry is not adventitious but integral to the Church's existence; of this the New Testament leaves us in no doubt whatsoever.

The Concept of a Necessary Ministry

There is nothing subchristian in this conviction, although some writers would appear to think so. The difficulty with those who dislike the idea of a necessary ministry would seem to be rooted in an insufficient emphasis on the incarnational and sacramental mode of God's operation, centrally exhibited in Christ Himself. Obviously *God* is not dependent upon any historical "conditions," upon any created thing, for His existence. In a sense, He is not dependent upon anything other than Himself for the accomplishment of His holy will. Yet He has chosen to reveal Himself in, to work through, and to employ for His purposes, a created order, of which—so far as our knowledge goes and at least on this planet—the crown is man. God moves in and through man as the ground and principle of man's being. Above all, He *becomes Man,* in Jesus Christ—a Jew of Palestine. By this act He incorporates men, in whom He is already present both by the Word and by the Holy Spirit, into the divine-human life of His incarnate Son and makes them, by that fact, "partakers of the divine nature." All of this is done in historic, human terms.

It is consonant with this mode of operation, and in that sense it is altogether natural, that the way in which the Church should symbolize its identity is through some outward and visible means, acting sacramentally for the inner and spiritual reality of Christ's ongoing life in the world, and thereby acting sacramentally for the whole reality of the Church as the militant, expectant, and triumphant community of those who have been grafted into Christ, with Christ Himself as their living Head through the Holy Spirit. If Bishop Stephen Neill feels that insistence on the ministry, seen in this light, is based upon a different idea of God from that which he thinks the Gospel teaches, we can only conclude that at this point he has misunderstood the Gospel.[8]

If this view be taken seriously, it can be maintained, with no subtraction from the sublimity of the Church's nature and with no sullying of that nature by materiality more serious than the sullying which God Himself willed and endured by the Incarnation, that the ministry in its true character is indeed functional, but that it is functional in a genuine, that is an ontological, sense. That is to say, it is intrinsic to and persistent in the ontological reality of the Church with its inner being established by God through

His incarnate action. Hence the ministry is also ontological and necessary, rather than accidental.

It is important, of course, to make certain immediate qualifications at this point, lest we relapse into the earlier error, namely, that the ministry has a status that is so necessary that once again it is thought of as "making" the Church. To hold the balance is perhaps a difficult, but it is not an impossible, task. There is but one ministry which is the absolute *prius* to all other ministries; it is the ministry of Jesus Christ, divine and human, High Priest and Mediator beween God and His children, which not only must always be placed first but must also be made central in our understanding of the Church's ministerial expression. Christ is the incarnate Word of God; as such He is the eternal as well as the historical grounding of the ministry of the Church as well as of the Church in which the ministry is found. It is from Him that the Church derives its being; He is the Head of His Body. It is from Him, too, that all ministry takes its origin. Nothing which has so far been argued would deny that Christ is the first and true minister in all ministry. The Church's ministry derives from Him, but it derives from Him in and through His mystical Body.

The Reconciliation of Divergent Concepts

It is our contention, then, that there is no real contradiction between the two statements: "All ministry is directly derived from Christ," and "All ministry is functional to the life of the Church." The only way in which such a contradiction could arise would be from a failure to grasp the permanent truth that Christ is ever Lord over His Church as well as over the very Life of that Church, which is His Body and in which, as Head, He is the informing principle, through the responsive work of the Holy Spirit of God. We may put it bluntly: to say that the Church's inner reality is the precondition for all ministry, is simply to say that Christ Himself is the precondition. For He, and He *only*, is the inner Reality of the Church in the true and ultimate sense of that phrase.

In this way we should seek to correct the errors to which we have called attention. And in correcting them, we maintain the truth which each has at heart, but which each has imperfectly expressed because it has forgotten the other side of the picture. As so frequently happens in theological discussions, the trouble comes when a particular idea is held out of relation to balancing ideas; the consequence of such a one-sided grasp of truth is that the very point which is being stressed is so disproportionately asserted that it becomes actual error. In the matter here under consideration, it would seem that the mistaken insistence upon single elements, without their balancing opposites, has in fact led to very grievous error.

The Mode of Divine Action

Those of us who were privileged over many years to enjoy daily conversation with Dr. Hughell E. W. Fosbroke, for thirty years Dean of the General Theological Seminary in New York, recall that there were two things on which he always insisted. In all deeply Christian thought, Dr. Fosbroke used to say, there can never be any question concerning the priority of the divine action over all human activity. God is *first* and it is God who initiates, sometimes openly and sometimes secretly. The doctrine of prevenience is an indispensable element in Christian thinking. Human action is, therefore, responsive; it is reaction to the divine action. But on the other hand, Dr. Fosbroke insisted, it is also true that God is at work in the "horizontal" level of nature and history. The divine action is not only from above downwards to creation, as it were "vertically"; it is also along the level of the created order itself. This does not imply any simple "progressist" view of history; it is concerned only to maintain that God is genuinely at work in His world, and that the events which take place in that world are meaningful in their constant relationship to the divine action.

Now many theologians would appear to regard these two ideas as so contradictory that they are obliged to choose one of them to the exclusion of the other. Hence we find overemphasis on transcendence or overemphasis on immanence. Hence we are asked to choose one side or another in regard to God's revelation and about His work in redemption: either this must be divine operation *or* this must be human operation. But as Dr. Fosbroke insisted, and as we should insist after him, the sound Christian view is that the two ideas, while not patient of any easy reconciliation, must yet be held together, for both are required in any adequate interpretation of the facts of life and experience, not only within but also outside the saving communion with God which Christ makes possible for men.

The Principle Applied to the Ministry

The principle here enunciated has its very pointed application to the ministry of the Church. That ministry, insofar as it is *Christ's* ministry, stands for and effectually symbolizes the divine action in and through the Church as the Body of Christ. The ministry is from God through His incarnate Son, through His Body the Church, and *in* His Body the Church. But insofar as the ministry is by that token the *Church's* ministry, it has continuity with the past and from the historian's point of view is itself a product of that past. It probably emerges, as we shall seek to show, from the ancient Jewish pattern which was taken over and employed by the earliest Christians who sought to establish, under God and through the Holy Spirit, the new fellowship among the peoples of the world. In response to the insistent pressure of events and circumstances, as the community moved out into the Gentile world, the ministry moulded itself so that it took on a certain structure. The process was obviously one of development; but as it went forward, the ministry was increasingly recognized and asserted to be intrinsic to the continuity of the Christian society, for it was seen to "externalize" and in a sacramental manner make real the historical development itself. With all of its change and in all of its growth it was yet one with itself, continuous with the earliest years of Christianity and carrying on the same work in the world.

In other words, it is improper to set up the terms, "from God" and "historically developed," as if they were absolutely opposed the one to the other. Both terms are in accord with the facts and both terms must be maintained. The ministry is from God *and* it has been historically developed. How else, indeed, could the Church's order—or anything else, for that matter—come from God, unless it came through the realm of event and in interaction with the whole rich complex of happening which we call "history"? Any other interpretation would seem to land us in a view of revelation which can no longer be maintained and which, indeed, is contrary to the scriptural picture—we have no evidence whatsoever for the notion that God acts upon men solely and utterly *ab extra,* dropping propositions and institutions from heaven without regard for the time-and-space situation of His human children and their natural mode of apprehension of truth.

Summary

The continual union of divine action and human action, the latter responsive to the former, is seen supremely when we look at the whole picture through eyes that have seen the glory of God in the face of Jesus Christ. For in the light of the Incarnation, we know that God's vertical action is horizontally expressed. The fulness of grace and truth, which came by Jesus Christ, dwelt among us in the limitations of a human life and experience; yet the "conditioning" factor did not simply obscure the reality of God's action, but rather was the way in which that reality was made operative upon the field of history, the only way in which it *could* become operative—namely, *ad modum recipientis.* God in His gracious humility wills to accommodate Himself to our time-and-space "poverty"; in so doing, He reveals among other things that our time-and-space "poverty" is not really such at all. On the contrary, it is the divinely-given abode in which we live as men; it is a good world, though it is finite and though it can be made "miserable" for us by our sin. Yet its very conditions, once we live in faith, can also become (like Isaiah's mountains) "a way" by which we travel to our true *patria* in God.

These considerations, drawn from the realm of Christological and soteriological thought, have their relevance to the field of ecclesiology and to the "holy order" of the Church. We need not be afraid that we shall degrade Christian truth when we insist that a ministry which is historically "conditioned," and which by its very nature involves such material forms as particular words of ordination, is symbol and sign of the Church as the Bride of Christ, His Spouse and His Body. To be afraid of such "degradation" is to be more refined than God Himself.

Before we consider the nature of the Christian ministry in its relation to the Church as the Spirit-indwelt Body of Christ, we must discuss certain questions that have a serious bearing on the problem. The first point is the general way in which the Church has developed its "organic structure." This we shall consider in the next chapter. The other important matter is the actual historical situation so far as the question of "origins" of the ministry is concerned. To this we shall turn in the third chapter.

There is a distinction, let it be noted, between these questions. The first involves a wide consideration of the relationship of the Body to its "structures," seen in historical perspective. The second calls for a study of the concrete facts which illuminate the ministry in its persistence through change in the early days of the Christian community. We shall not be able to give an absolutely certain account of "origins." Much of the work which has been done in this field is tentative and the conclusions have at best only a high degree of probability. Harm can only come from claiming too much in this area. What is clear to us is what in fact did *emerge* from the primitive and early period, and it is upon this that we shall lay stress. For it is this which, in our judgment, gives us the necessary clue to the nature of the ministry and its proper function in the Church's life.

Abbé Loisy once remarked that one does not prove the identity of a man with his own infancy by attempting to push him back into his perambulator. Development implies change but does not necessarily mean a loss of selfhood. Selfhood is not demonstrated by finding explicitly in the baby all that is later seen in the fullgrown man. We must say that without subscribing to Loisy's eccentric and now generally rejected ideas of the origins of Christianity, this point is as true of the Church's ministry as it is of everything else in the Christian tradition. The way to approach our problem, historically, is by the analytical method, in which the later emergent is used as a means for understanding the sources. If these sources should quite definitely *contradict* the emergent, we can be sure that something is wrong; if, however, there is a genuine congruity between them, we may well believe that the emergent should be "received and believed," since it has been "proved"—that is to say, "tested"—by the primitive Christian life and experience, and is thus grounded upon the faith and life of the Christian Church in its formative, and in that sense its normative, period.

II

THE DEVELOPING LIFE OF THE BODY

OF CHRIST

———

THE Church is the Body of Christ. It is no amorphous or invertebrate entity; it is an integrated and truly organic unity. It is impossible to dispute the fact that such a conception of the Church prevailed in the apostolic age; it is also certain that in the succeeding years of Christian history, the great theologies have consistently held that the Church is a divinely created society, not the invention of men. While it is true that at one time or another, and sometimes for long periods, the Church has been regarded in a legalistic or even a mechanical way, over and over again there have come "times of refreshing" when the vital energies which dwell in the Church have reasserted themselves and men have been obliged to reckon with the fact that here is indeed a *Body*, with a wonderful capacity to revive; a *Vine*, which is able to put forth fresh branches. The Church's vitality is demonstrated by its ability to live despite apparent death, with an eternal youth as well as an ancient wisdom.

It is now generally agreed by theologians, whether they are of Protestant or Catholic background, that the Church came into being through the impact of the event of Christ upon the older Israel, the community into which He was born and in which He lived and taught. The late Archbishop William Temple once pointed out that when the historic Jesus ended His days in the flesh, He left behind Him, not a doctrine nor an ethic, but a society in which He was still present and through which He still worked among men. From the womb of "Israel after the flesh," from the Jewish nation and People, there was born "Israel after the Spirit," the Christian Church. In response to the action of God, the Word incarnate in man, there emerged, through the operation of the Holy Ghost, the divine society, which the writers of the New Testament did not hesitate to describe in what we should call organic terms. To be a Christian meant, for St. Paul, to be "in Christ"; and to be "in Christ" meant, for the same apostle, to belong to the Body of Christ as a living member of the same.

The Divine Society in the New Testament

The author of St. John's Gospel clearly has this idea in mind, although he does not employ the particular metaphor of body and members. When he speaks of the vine and the branches, he is saying that to belong to Christ, who is for him the *Logos* enfleshed, is to be a branch in the Vine which is Christ Himself. The life of the Vine is Christ's own life. Indeed, the Vine itself is so to be understood as Christ, with those incorporated into Him as "branches," that those who are branches of the Vine are by that token sharers, in the deepest sense, in the very being of God the Word, made flesh in the Man Jesus. Still another classical statement of this set of ideas may be found in the Epistle to the Ephesians, where the unknown author takes Pauline notions and develops them more fully, maintaining that in the "one Body," with its "one Lord, one faith, one baptism," those who are called are being perfected, so that they are "saints" or "holy ones in the Lord," and in this great reality of the Church, which is being built-up by Christ through His Spirit, the Lord is bringing into Himself the race of men. As men are redeemed, they are so "oned" with Christ that in the end there will be Christ-in-His-Church as a unity of Head and Body. St. Augustine put it in a phrase: Christ is *caput et corpus.*

In the First Epistle attributed to St. Peter, we find another clear expression of this view. Here Christians are asserted to constitute a royal priesthood and a chosen nation after the fashion of the earlier Israel. They are a people peculiar or unique in that they have been called in Christ, and by Him have been constituted as God's new race; they are "lively stones" built up as a "spiritual house" in which God dwells through Christ by the Spirit. With whatever variations we may find in statement or detail, there can be no doubt that all of these writers, and others in the New Testament, hold the same general view of the meaning of Christian discipleship: for them all, to be of Christ is to be of the Church, for Christ and His Church cannot be separated.

This then is the Divine Society, whose unity of life is in Christ, indeed *is* Christ. But on the other hand, the response which was made, through the Holy Spirit, to the initial and continuing presence of God in Christ was not marked by a simple, as it were mathematical, unity. It was a unity of response which was rich and complex, like the unity that we know in natural and human organic life, where the various parts and members are held together as one by their common response to the environment or to some stimulus playing upon them, yet at the same time retain their rich variety and differentiation. This is one of the reasons that the description of the Church as the Body of Christ is so remarkably apt; whatever explains its original use by St. Paul and others, it can readily be seen that it safeguards and states, better than any other metaphor, the unity yet the complexity of the Church as it constantly responds to the divine work upon it and within it.

The Response of the Church to the Holy Spirit

The response to which we have just referred found itself articulated into several distinguishable "structures." These may well be regarded as the marks of the Church's continuous and identical life. We shall make certain general comments about these "structures" before we proceed to a more detailed examination of their development.

First of all, there was the *response in faith*. This response is seen in the affirmation of the Gospel, or (as the New Testament calls it) the *kerygma* or proclamation of God's redemptive act in Jesus Christ. The declaring of Christ's coming after a divine preparation of the Jewish people, of His life and death, of His resurrection and ascension, of

His expected return in judgment and consummation: here is the first response to Christ. Secondly, there was the *response in worship*. The Eucharist, in which the first Christians believed that they obeyed their Lord's command, "Do this in remembrance of me," was the way in which the body of believers "showed forth the Lord's death" and shared in "the communion of the body and blood of Christ." It was the characteristic element in this response in worship. Thirdly, there was the *response in life*—the empowering of man's whole being through his new "en-Christed" relationship to God. The fruit of the Spirit was manifested as the Christian let himself be formed by the life of the fellowship, and thus conformed to Christ who, as the community's Lord, was the pattern of the perfection to which he had been called.

But there was another structure which articulated itself in the Church's total response to the impact of Christ upon men. This was *holy order*, the ministerial expression of the Church's responding life. In our next chapter we shall give particular attention to this structure and consider historically its earliest stages and its redevelopment from them. At this point we wish merely to indicate that it was certainly there and that it would be a very arbitrary step to rule it out as secondary or irrelevant in the whole rich complex. The historic fact is that each of these "structures" is found in the New Testament; and the very writing of the books which constitute that document is itself the work of a community which knew all four of these "structures."

None of them came into being without a period of development. It was a defect in much of the earlier and pre-critical reading of the story that it assumed that the Christian faith, the worship of the Christian Church, its life in grace, and its ministerial ordering, could be found in a full-grown form, or at least in some fairly precise and definite form, in the New Testament itself. This can no longer be maintained. On the contrary, what we can affirm is that we discover in the most primitive material the germs from which these "structures" developed into their full flower. On the other hand, we are now able to see that none of them came into existence, in the life of the Church, as a sudden and arbitrary importation from outside into the vital Christian tradition. The theory that the "structures" were taken over, almost if not entirely, in their developed form from Hellenistic religion or from the mystery cults or from some other source, is now discredited. But there is no question that the "structures" of the Christian community must be traced as emerging from an early and inchoate form into the more richly developed form which the early community knew, and at length, through a period of controversy and growing understanding, into the full expression which at a relatively early date became normative for the Church.

Christianity as Tradition

Nor is the fact of this matter of development to be regarded with surprise. In the days when the Christian "way" burst upon the world, there was too much of a "first, fine, careless, rapture" for its implications to be drawn out and put forward in an explicit and defined fashion. It required the experience of several generations of believers, living the Christian life on the basis of the Gospel which was at the heart of the Christian story, nourished by the worship in which Christ's significance was established and His benefits shared by His redeemed followers, to bring the meaning of these things into a clear focus. If we remember that no absolute contradiction can be set up between "from God" and "historically developed," we shall find that this growth is no unnatural thing, but is, indeed, exactly what we should expect to have occurred. The Christian tradition, when it was in a form that could in fact be handed on *as* tradition, had acquired a characteristic "type" or quality of its own; the period before this crystallization may be compared to those early days in the life of a child when his implicit nature is being shaped and moulded so that his unique characteristics may be understood and appreciated.

In the faith of the Church, for example, there was unquestioned development from the earliest days. It required some considerable time for the faith in Jesus as "Word-made-flesh" to work itself out as the only adequate interpretation of His person. This is the case whether or not our Lord proclaimed Himself to be the expected Messiah of the Jews, or even taught His disciples privately that such was His true character. According to the reconstruction which to some of us seems most likely, the first Christian teaching about Jesus, as distinct from whatever appraisal of Him may have been made within the strictly Jewish context of His life and teaching in the days of His flesh, comes as a consequence of the experiences which we call the Resurrection. Jesus the teacher from Nazareth, who had been apprehended during His ministry as at the least "a prophet like unto Moses," had been put to death. And yet "this Jesus, whom ye crucified, God hath made him both Lord and Christ." It would appear obvious that the gospel record is coloured by the faith of the early believers whose traditions about Jesus it incorporated; the whole story was told of One who was known to have risen from the dead. However we may conceive of this indisputable central element in the primitive Christian assertion, it is this which made the faith in His messiahship a living and meaningful reality for His disciples.

And once it came to be believed that no categories less than the messianic were adequate to describe His significance, the Church was immediately prepared to penetrate even more deeply into the secret of Christ and soon was led to discover that even messiahship would not serve to explain Him who had brought life and immortality to light. If He could not be described in terms *less* than the messianic, neither could He be *contained* within these. He must be greater even than Messiah, even though the Messiah might be thought of in the "Son of Man" concept used to describe One who was "from heaven," and not a princely Davidic Messiah. Thus the thinkers of the early Christian Church, working with the material which they found in the given tradition of oral teaching about the Lord but much more dependent upon their own experience of life in the fellowship of which the Lord was the very centre and heart, were obliged to go further. St. Paul shows us what happened. From his conversion to the primitive Christian conviction of the messiahship of Jesus, he moved on within comparatively few years to the high Christology which is found expressed in no uncertain terms in the Epistle to the Romans. Finally, as shown by his teaching in the Epistle to the Colossians, he could use language which will admit of no other interpretation than that, for St. Paul, Jesus is the very act of God for human salvation.

From St. Paul there is a straight line to the Christology of the Fourth Gospel, no matter what other influences may have been brought to bear on Christian thought. Here our Lord is equated with the "Word," Deity in His out-going or self-expressive mode. Whatever may be the sources of the Johannine *Logos*-theology, the ideas are used as a way of stating the significance of the historic Jesus now known as the Christ of faith; Jesus is represented as speaking and acting in full consciousness of His being the Eternal Word. Although this divine self-consciousness is doubtless not true to the actual facts of history, it is true to the depths of Christian experience, which knew that out of the profound mystery of the transcendent Godhead Jesus Christ had emerged as "the way, the truth, and the life," and that in Him dwelt the "grace and truth" by which men come to the Father.

The Nicene Formulation

Given the necessary time and the opportunity to discover what may and must be involved in such a position ascribed to Jesus, the Nicene formulation, with its further clarification in the Chalcedonian definition, inevitably followed. Opposition from the pagan world, the insidious effort of some misguided persons to interpret Jesus in Gnostic terms, the pressure of persecution in which Jesus was found again to be Saviour from the evil of the world, made it imperative that the Church enter more and more searchingly into the meaning of that which it already knew as its vital faith. Thus Jesus was defined in the familiar terms as "very God of the substance of the Father; very Man of the substance of the Virgin Mary His Mother." This central Christological affirmation carried with it the whole trinitarian faith in God and His work amongst men, as later development was to demonstrate. It involved also a set of beliefs about the nature of the world in which men lived, the nature of the men whom God had created and whom He willed to redeem, and the ultimate destiny of men and the final goal of the created order under God's governance.

The Gospel, which is the proclamation that in Christ God has acted humanwise to save men, is then expressed in the dogma of the Incarnation. This is a minimal "form" for the safeguarding of the Church's integral life in faith, for the Incarnation with all that follows from it must be taken as the illumination of man's understanding of God, of himself, and of his world; while the Atonement gives a profounder grasp on the nature of man and his sinfulness, and the nature of God and His redeeming love for sinners. All of this explains why there is a Church at all. This is the apostolic faith, the first of the "structures" in the response of the Christian community to the impact of Christ upon the world. Even if we think (as we must) that the classical definitions are inadequate, imperfect, and in some respects mistaken, the total movement which led to them can be seen as necessary and right; and that movement provides the starting place for any restatement of the meaning of Christ in terms more congenial to our own age.

The Worship of the Christian Community

We have said that the second articulation in "structure" came in the worship of the Christian community. Here again we may trace a considerable development. There is no possibility of discovering in the New Testament record the full-grown eucharistic worship which is described, say, by Justin Martyr in his *Apology*. Yet granted the principle of development, it was such eucharistic worship that necessarily emerged from the picture of Christianity about which we read in Acts and in the Epistles. The Last Supper with His disciples, when Jesus gave to the common Jewish experience of the breaking of bread and the sharing of the cup, the new significance of His self-offering for His people, is the first step. We move on through the eucharistic *anamnesis* of Christ's passion in the days of the primitive community (as sketched, for example, in St. Paul's First Epistle to the Corinthians: 10:16-17; 11:23-29), to the completely explicit Christian Eucharist in the days of Justin. Here again we have a straight line of growth. But as Dom Gregory Dix and others have shown, there is in this process a continuity in eucharistic idea, as well as in fundamental liturgical structure, both of which show the identity of meaning in the rite from the earliest days to the later period.

The mystery religions of the Hellenistic world might, and possibly did, influence the details in this development of the Eucharist; in any event, as Dr. A. D. Nock has demonstrated in his remarkable study *Conversion,* Christianity conquered the world as a "mystery." But this must not be pressed beyond the patent fact that it offered in explicit reality that which was suggested and partially given in these cults. There can be no doubt that it was by no artificial importation into Christianity from outside the growing tradition, but by the Last Supper itself as continued in the eucharistic action, that eventually the Christian Church adopted the full Christian conception of the meaning of this action. Obviously it may have been brought into clearer focus by many other influences; but here once again we see through the passing years the articulation of the primitive Christian "way."

The Church had the *why* of its existence in the apostolic faith; it found the liturgical expression of that existence when it gathered for the sacramental observance which the Anglican Prayer Book, in language that is strictly true to the scriptural picture, calls "the continual remembrance of the sacrifice of the death of Christ." If there was any one thing done, which by being done indicated the unbroken unity and continuity of the Christian faithful, it was to be found in the unfailing gathering-together of the flock for the purpose of "showing forth the Lord's death." This was the Church's apostolic worship, appearing in the response of the community to the impact of Christ.

In neither of these structures can we push back the completed response, in all its richness, into the New Testament record. Yet both the completed Christian faith and the completed mode of worship of God are to be found germinally in our earliest historical materials. If we are prepared to grant that the faith which is stated for us in that apostolic record has any validity, we shall be ready to see that it was inevitable that it would develop with the years, bringing into greater clarity the implications which were within it. So also the Church found a more adequate expression of these implications as its contact with a pagan environment and its own deepening meditation on the significance of its experience, led it to work out what Christianity really meant in and of itself. This is perhaps nowhere so clear as in the third of the "structures" which we are discussing: the Christian "life."

Of course, the specific Christian ethic is *indicated* to us in the teaching of Jesus Himself, as well as in the exhortations and admonitions of the apostles—especially, perhaps, in the writings of St. Paul and the author of the Johannine literature. Yet it required fuller experience of life in the grace of the Lord Jesus, fuller contact with the life thought of the non-Christian world, to make it possible to work out in any detail that which was involved in the fact that the believer no longer lived "unto himself" but found his life "in Christ."

The Early Conception of Christian Life

This third articulation, then, was the realization and the explication of the experienced fact that to be a member of the Christian community, incorporated into the Body of Christ, meant to have introduced into one's life a new principle of being, to be caught up into another realm, and to live—potentially and to an increasing degree, actually—through the sanctifying power of the Holy Ghost. Life must be seen and lived in terms of the new reality to which one now belonged. The relationship which one sustained to God and to one's fellows, in consequence of incorporation with Christ, was "en-graced." And this was something very different from "following the ethical teaching of Jesus"; it was, if you will, an ontological, rather than a merely ethical, situation.

The earliest conception of the Christian life was undoubtedly based on the obedience which the disciple owed to the teaching of Jesus, now understood as the Messiah, concerning the proper way of observing the Jewish Law. This was the new "yoke," which our Lord said was "easy, and its burden light." For the first Christian disciples, in the sense of the immediate followers of the Nazarene, this must have meant deliverance from the picayune detail and the hidebound moral traditionalism of the scribes and the Pharisees. But it was not until the fact of Jesus as risen from the dead, and hence known as a life-giving Spirit, came vividly alive in the experience of the primitive community that the unique quality of the Christian life became an ex-

plicit reality. We can see this happening in the experience
of St. Paul himself. No longer was it enough to portray
the moral life of the Christian as being in effect "the right
way of obeying the Law." Christian morality meant life
in the Spirit, or life in Christ.

For those who had dwelling within them the very life of
the risen Messiah—or, better stated, for those who because
they shared in "the fellowship of the Holy Spirit" could
know "the grace of the Lord Jesus Christ" and thereby be
assured of "the love of God," as St. Paul puts it in II Corinthians—there was no longer any thought of mere obedience
to the Law. The Law, as the ancient moral code which must
be carefully followed by the pious Jew, was supplanted by
the Spirit of life in Jesus Christ. Of course, the Law was
not dead. It still stood, as St. Paul insisted in Romans, as
the judgment of God upon men, and upon each man, for
failure to do the will of God. But Christian life is something
else.

There were lapses from this new understanding of freedom in the grace of Christ. Part of the *Didache,* for example, as well as other early Christian writings like the
letters of Clement of Rome and the *Shepherd of Hermas,*
seem to return to the older view. But where one finds a
profound understanding of the work of Christ, as expressed
in such documents as the *Epistle to Diognetus,* in parts of
Justin Martyr, and in Ignatius of Antioch with his complete absorption in the Lord who is his "love," one sees
that the new fact has been applied to life. Later, when one
comes upon the deep insight of Clement of Alexandria, of

Origen, and others like them, the new reality of life in Christ is known to have been apprehended and experienced. And if this is true in the literature of this early period, how much more true it must have been in the experience of simple believers—the kind described by St. Paul as neither mighty nor noble, in the world's eyes. They found themselves delivered both from the rigidity of the Jewish law into the freedom wherewith Christ makes men free, and from the sensuality and libertinism of the pagan world into the ordered liberty in the Spirit, which brought forth the fruit of the Spirit in "love, joy, peace, long-suffering, gentleness, goodness, faith, meekness, temperance" (Galatians 5:22-23). It was in truth, as the Johannine writer put it, like coming out of darkness into light.

Once more then, we have seen a development in understanding, following upon an explication of the apprehended meaning of the Christian "way." Here was the growing expression of what was implied in deliverance from triviality and frustration into meaningful life and devoted service. This is the significance of the apostolic life as it was known in the community of faith.

The Parallel Development of the Ministry

But why, we may be asked, should there be such an extended exposition of the development of Christian faith, worship, and life in a book that is concerned with the Christian ministry? The answer to this question ought to be plain. The ministry itself developed like these other three "structures" of the Christian Church. No one of the four can be separated from the other three. They all had their roots in the same historical situation, they all emerged from the same Jewish background, they all had their further explication in reaction to the same pagan and Hellenistic world. Most important of all, they all had their meaning in terms of the same total response in the Holy Spirit to the work of God in Christ. The development was not, of course, entirely equal, point by point. In fact, the ministry emerged in fairly explicit form before the faith reached its Nicene statement, and practically coterminously with the eucharistic worship of the Church. But they are not separate and separable entities; they are a closely-entwined rope which must be kept together if any one of them is to be rightly known.

The significance of this discussion is that it has indicated for us the way in which the historical *datum* has actually been used in the Christian community. Christianity is not a hidebound tradition, which must always return to the precise formulations, the exact sets of ideas, the same practices and habits which were inculcated in its earliest days. Rather, Christianity is a living tradition which grows out of historical events; it grows out of them, but it does not leave them behind. That which actually was wrought out by God in history, that which the events mean, that which they have implied, that which they have introduced into the experience of men—all these are conserved in the on-going movement. But the tradition must and does move.

It works out, in the light of a deepening experience and a more penetrating understanding, what the history suggests and means.

Surely it would be absurd to insist that Christian dogma can have no statement in any form other than that which is contained within the pattern of words found in the pages of the New Testament. Even more absurd would it be to demand that the theological expression of the Christian faith must be identical not only with the pattern of words but with the *ipsissima verba* of the New Testament writers. Every church historian knows that this kind of thinking is more characteristic of Arian mentality than of the thought of those who, like St. Athanasius, saw that it was imperative to use other than scriptural words in order to preserve the genuine significance of the Gospel itself. St. Athanasius fought a battle "against the world" to make this clear. Hence his insistence upon the insertion, at Nicaea, of the *homoousion* ("of one substance with the Father") into the Church's credal affirmation. In the same way, there is something absurd in attempts to make Christian worship in succeeding centuries an exact imitation of the action and words in the Upper Room at the Last Supper. Nor is Christian morality the literal following of the exact words of Jesus or of the New Testament writers; it is the participation in the Spirit of Christ as He lives in the world today. There is change at every point. And yet there is also identity. The line of development is clear; the *direction* of change is plain. It is not sheer exuberant, uncontrolled vital energy, but a directed and channeled energy, with what we may call (in a misuse of Mr. Clive Bell's phrase) a "significant form."

So likewise it must be, and so it is, with the Church's ministry. The attempt to push the developing "order" or the Body of Christ back into a precise New Testament pattern, even if that pattern could be recovered, would be entirely beside the point. It is indeed necessary to study the evidence, and to seek to discover, as the result of a reading of the early documentary evidence, the primitive ministry of the Church; but to assume that from this study an established form of ministry which flourished universally during the first few decades of apostolic history can be recovered, is essentially unrealistic. The study of the material is of vast importance; but by the very nature of the material it can never be conclusive. There was change, there was development, after the New Testament and the first Christian days. On the other hand, there was continuity. This continuity, as we shall argue in our next chapter, was one of function and not one of nomenclature; the continuity was in the work done and in the existence of agents to do it. But what we might call the "arrangements of the ministry," and the specific names by which the different "officers" were called, did not necessarily continue the same.

The Apostolic Ministry

Thus we may rightly say that the fourth mode or articulation in the Christian response, in the divine society, to the ingression of God in Christ, was the ministry which is properly called "apostolic." That means that there was an ordering of the community, however germinal in form, such as the Anglican Prayer Book in its Ordinal describes as existing "from the Apostles' time." But it cannot be claimed that the description of that ministry in a threefold form, bishops-priests-deacons, is an accurate description. There is no sufficient reason, on the basis of the evidence, to push the later "arrangements" of the apostolic ministry back into the New Testament itself. But we have seen that such an attempt would in any event be disloyal to the genius of the Christian community's existence. On the other hand, there is quite adequate evidence for the sort of continuity which we have maintained is necessary. There are the germinal beginnings of such a ministry in the New Testament and in primitive Christian times; and it is from such beginnings, found there in germinal form, that the Christian Church worked out its "order" into that shape which became normative for the Church as it continued down the centuries.

In each of these four structures we can see the truth of the contention which was made in the opening chapter of this book. The faith, the worship, the life-in-grace, the ministry, are, indeed, all "from above." That is, they are all divinely "instituted" in that they came into being as the response to the action of God in Christ, as by the Holy Spirit the Christian community found life in Him. On the other hand, they are all "historically developed." They take their explicit form through the vicissitudes of historical happening, in contact with the events in time and space, through that interaction of man with man, and man with circumstance, which is what we mean when we talk of the realm of the historical.[1]

The Necessary Element of History

We contend that there is a *necessary* element of genuine history in the whole Christian complex; without that "historical happenedness," as Baron von Hügel put it, there would be and could be no Christianity. Yet we should insist that we learn the meaning of that which historically has occurred when we see what it has meant and still means in the continuing life of the fellowship which it brought into being. Further, we know what we do know of the historical facts only through the Christian community which gave "eyes of faith" to those who preserved the earliest records. There is no such thing, in the Christian religion, as "uninterpreted" or completely "objective" historical data. But it would involve a prolonged discussion if we were to demonstrate the point; reference may be made to the admirable treatment of this problem of our knowledge of the historical material in the opening chapters of Dr. F. C. Grant's recent *Introduction to New Testament Thought*.

For our particular purpose, this "community-conveyance" of the historical event is especially significant. It is true of the faith, of the worship, of the Christian life-in-grace; it is equally true of the ministry. Rooted in the New Testament evidence, in that its germinal beginnings are there, it required the events of history, the contact with the pagan world, the growing demands of the Church's own life for organization and formalization, before its real meaning could be sufficiently explicated. That is why it took time. But to take time does not mean to render unhistorical or irrelevant. It means to show what is in fact involved. It is our contention that the ministry which at last emerged, within not much more than one hundred years, is rightly to be accepted as the normative ministry of the Christian Church. It has an a priori claim upon us for our acceptance as the proper ministry of the Church, just as the faith which was stated at Nicaea and Chalcedon, the worship which became regularized at a much earlier period than that, and the understanding of the meaning of the new life in Christ which flowered during the Roman Empire's persecutions of the Church, have their a priori claim upon those who would be in the mainstream of historical Christian development.

It must certainly be granted that from time to time there may be a new grasp of the implications of the faith, worship, and life of the Christian Church. But such a new grasp is not to be won by an attempt to *reverse* the historical process; rather it is to be discovered in the full and grateful use of that which we have received. To *go back* to some presumed prior ministry is very near to being blasphemy against God the Holy Ghost; while to trust the ministry as we have received it, to use it to the fullest, to show willingness to share it with others, and to seek to understand what it may imply and how it may be developed in the years to come, is to put one's confidence in the Holy Spirit's guidance of Christ's Catholic Church, taking "the things of Christ" and showing them unto us.

III

THE HISTORICAL BACKGROUND

OF THE MINISTRY

WITHIN the past few decades renewed interest has been shown in the problem of the origins of the Christian ministry. The result of this research is that some questions which previously had been serious obstacles to our understanding of the development of the ministry in its earlier days have been answered; others have to some degree been modified. We now have a much better picture of the actual historical situation. We are able to see something of the relation of the later Christian ministry to the Jesus of history; even more surely we can understand the relation of the ministry of the Christian Church to the Jewish social and religious pattern out of which Christianity itself emerged.

Yet absolute certainty on details of the primitive ministry has not been attained; and it is unlikely that we shall ever have enough information to trace fully the whole developing pattern. Some of the earliest evidence which would be of primary importance is lost and can never be recovered. Much of the material which is available can be interpreted in different ways. And we still have, and are likely to continue to have a dark or "tunnel" period between the close of the apostolic age and the emergence into the open daylight, some fifty years later, of the fairly regularly ordered ministry—the ministry which the Anglican Prayer Book correctly describes as existing in the Church through the succeeding centuries: bishops, priests, and deacons. Perhaps the "tunnel" is not now quite so dark as once it was; there is some evidence as to what went into it at one end, and we know what came out of it at the other end. But the whole story is by no means as plain as we should like.

Furthermore, the particular theological considerations which every scholar must entertain, no matter how "objective," he may profess to be, are bound to have their influence upon his findings. One's over-all appraisal of the meaning of the Church and the significance of the ministry as known today will necessarily have an effect on one's study. Indeed, even to have no special presuppositions, as might be the situation of a non-Christian historical expert, is already to have presuppositions; there can be no consideration of a fact without some implicit interpretation of the fact; and the idea of an utterly "pure" history, with no meaning of any sort whatsoever, is an illusion not only for those engaged in the investigation of so-called "religious" events but also for those working in the field of so-called "secular" events.

When, for example, H. A. L. Fisher in the preface to his great one-volume *History of Europe* professed that he found no meaning in the historical process, and therefore could see no purpose, aim, or value, but only event following event in the European scene, he was deluding himself and probably fooling many of his readers. A careful reading of his work indicates that he did indeed use an interpretative principle, unconsciously no doubt, and therefore did see a meaning in events: it was a movement towards the liberalism of a highly educated, sensitive Englishman, concerned for democratic values and intent upon that broadening of precedent and liberating of the spirit of man with which late Victorian, Edwardian, and early Georgian Englishmen seemed to identify the evolutionary process. Interpretation and meaning are inevitably involved as we study the past, even if we "smuggle" them in without any explicit awareness of what we are doing.

All this should make us proceed with caution in the attempt to sketch the historical background and development of the Christian ministry. But, on the other hand, it should not suggest to us that nothing worth discovering may come to hand. What is required is a reasonable humility in the face of facts, a willingness to look at these facts honestly even if they do not appear to be "in our favour," and a determination that we shall not press particular details to such a degree that the total picture is distorted.

The Relation of Christ and His Flock in the Gospel

The first factor which should be noted is that the Gospels unquestionably portray for us a relationship between Jesus Christ and His "flock," in which there is something like a representative principle at work. It is, of course, obvious that this must not be pushed to the point where it is claimed that our Lord was establishing, in detail and with precision, the program of a future ecclesiastical institution. Nobody today would assume that Jesus was drawing-up "blueprints" for the Church through the succeeding centuries. Our knowledge of the eschatological framework for His teaching would preclude our entertaining any such idea. What does emerge, however, from a broad consideration of the early oral traditions about the life and teaching of Jesus, as these traditions are given to us in the Gospels, is that when Jesus called to Him those whom He would have with Him, He chose certain members of the company and placed them in a particular relationship with Himself. These constituted what might be called "the inner circle," the group known as "the Twelve." To them He seems to have opened His heart and shared His mind in a fashion quite different from that in which He taught and worked with the larger group of those who heard His preaching of the kingdom. Exactly what function "the Twelve" may have had is not entirely clear in the detail which we might wish, but it seems certain that they were, at the least, the confidants and the constant companions of the Lord, as He went about Palestine with them, on His mission of preaching and healing. It also appears that they were expected in some sense to "act" for him, both in preaching and in healing and exorcism.

Certain writers have given great importance to the Jewish conception of the "shaliach" prevalent in Christ's day.

The "shaliach" was a representative, fully empowered to act for the one whom he represented. His action was said to "bind" his principal, so that the saying, "A man's 'shaliach' is as himself," was a familiar one. This idea of the "shaliach" is, indeed, found in material of the rabbinical period of Judaism and unquestionably has a considerable significance. But some scholars have assumed that the relation of the intimate band of Jesus' disciples to their Lord must necessarily have been moulded after this pattern. They have paid especial attention to the "shaliach" of the High Priest or of the Great Sanhedrin; and they have contended that this office could be, and almost certainly was, extended to include representation of other than these high dignitaries. They have used this idea with a confidence hardly warranted by the facts of which we are in possession. It may be correct to say that the notion of the "shaliachate" was widespread at the time of Jesus' ministry, although we have no evidence that this was so; but there is no reason to assume that the function of "the Twelve," in relation to Jesus, was precisely of this nature. There is insufficient material on this point to make it a safe assumption, although, doubtless, later Christian writers had the idea in mind. There seems at least no compelling reason to *equate,* as such writers seem to do, the term *apostolos,* which came to be applied to the leading Christian "mission-workers," if we may call them such, who carried on their work for Jesus as His "agents," with the Jewish "shaliach." There may indeed be evidence which points in this direction; but it is not safe to take it as conclusive.

What we may safely claim is that the immediate associates of Jesus, called "the Twelve," were uniquely His representatives in certain particular functions. They acted for Him in the preaching of the kingdom, and in healing and exorcism, in the days of His flesh. That they were "to him as if he himself were present," which as we have seen is the binding nature of the "shaliach" conception, is not equally clear. That they acted for Him is plain; that He was "bound" by their actions seems highly improbable. Indeed, in terms of later Christian belief in Jesus, it would deny that relationship of one-way dependence upon Jesus which the early Church, and indeed all sound Christian thought as well, has insisted in its view of God's work and man's instrumental agency on God's behalf.

Beyond "the Twelve" there were "the Seventy." What precisely can be made of this distinction is not obvious. But we may recognize that Jesus entrusted His work not only to an intimate band of followers, who constantly companied with Him, but also gave the task of preaching the kingdom and "casting out demons" to others who went through Palestine, on His behalf, announcing the Good News and winning followers to the new way of Jewish discipleship in the light of the advent of the kingdom. It is important to be clear that this first preaching and teaching did not concern Jesus Himself; it concerned the coming of God's kingdom of righteousness and the right manner of obedience to the Jewish Law. Jesus' "yoke was easy," His "burden was light." As contrasted with the meticulous, over-legalistic "yoke" and "burden" which

the scribes and Pharisees would impose upon the faithful
Jew, Jesus and those who spoke for Him put fellowship
with God at the heart of the religious life. They declared
that when men lived in expectation of the kingdom, the
powers of the kingdom were already present, and men
were in fact living in it, in faith and obedience, as the
will of their heavenly Father became the dominant principle of their living.

But this teaching, as generally given, had an important
corollary for those who were close to Jesus Himself. They
knew that in and with Him, the powers of the coming
age were already being released, so that where He was,
there the kingdom was present. Men not merely lived in
it, as they obeyed, in faith, its anticipated righteousness.
They also found it "coming upon them" when they experienced its powers in that which Jesus was and did. The
extent to which our Lord Himself taught this explicitly,
and the extent to which He made claims for Himself
which were then to be declared to others, is not clear. It
would seem, in any event, that He did not assert that
He was the Messiah in anything like the conventional
Jewish sense of a political figure; and we may even doubt
that He applied to Himself, without equivocation, the
notion of the heavenly Son of Man. What would appear
to be beyond question is that Jesus took upon Himself,
and even claimed for Himself, at least towards the close
of His ministry, such a place in God's purposes that He
was essential to the bringing-in of God's kingdom. He
believed that God had "sent" Him for this task, "chosen"

Him to carry out this work. Hence, through the preaching of the coming kingdom, through the enunciation of God's righteous and loving will for men, through the works of mercy, and in the end, as the event proved, through His willing acceptance of death, God's kingdom would be made a potent and living reality—as even now, in the days of His earthly ministry itself, it was "at hand" whenever it was preached and whenever its "powers" were manifested in works of healing and of exorcism.

"From Faith to Faith"

This would mean that the band who acted on Jesus' behalf, either as "the Twelve" or as "the Seventy," were in effect ministers not only for the preaching of the kingdom, but were also ministers of Jesus Himself. And those who were won to the new "way" through such preaching and through the "mighty works" which accompanied it were consciously related to Jesus as their Master. He was the "Lord," and they constituted a community with Him which made their leaders representative of the Master, who was for them so much more than merely "rabbi." Yet the group whom we call "the Twelve," like those whom we call "the Seventy," could never be said to "make" the community; it came into being through the work of Jesus Himself, and all who were in it were related to Him as their Master, carrying on for Him the several functions which were given them to do.

Now the difficulty, if indeed it be a difficulty, which we face in all of this discussion is that the Gospels cannot be understood, nor can they be interpreted, apart from the life of the primitive Christian community itself. Whatever may be the extremes to which advocates of the form-critical method of New Testament study have gone, one thing is quite plain. The picture of Jesus which we find in the Gospels is *the community's picture;* the whole account, as we have already insisted, was written "from faith to faith." Those who gave us the stories were themselves believers in the Lord. They knew Him to be not only the historic "prophet like unto Moses," as Acts implies, but also the Messiah, now risen and soon to return in glory. It was to impart this faith and to strengthen this conviction that they took the current oral tradition and from it made up an account of Jesus' life and teaching. As St. Mark's Gospel makes clear, in its very first words, the reason for writing down the oral traditions about Jesus was that believers might know of "the beginning"—that is, the actual origin in the events which had taken place—"of the glad proclamation of Jesus who is Messiah and Son of God." The Fourth Gospel puts the same point even more plainly: "These are written, that ye might believe that Jesus is the Christ, the Son of God; and that believing ye might have life through his name."

We have learned now not to make an easy and complete distinction between the Synoptic Gospels and the Fourth Gospel, such as was popular twenty to forty years ago. In a real sense, *all* of the gospel material is of the same sort. The degree of interpretation of fact, in the light of the dominant faith of the primitive community, may be enormously heightened; the factual element, as we like to call it, may be seriously modified; the first three Gospels may give us a more "accurate," although never a strictly "scientific-historical," account of what Jesus was like and what He did in the days of His flesh. But it remains an indisputable truth that the entire gospel record is mediated through the life in faith of the primitive Christian fellowship. We shall never understand what the actual events may have been like if we try to get at them apart from, or without regard for, the particular *stance* of the Evangelists and of the community whose oral traditions these Evangelists were setting down, modifying, employing for their own purposes. Even if, as with some of the miracles, we cannot agree with the Evangelists' view of the world and what is likely to happen in it, we must still put ourselves back into their situation if we are to have any knowledge of "those things which were most surely believed" among the faithful in the earliest days.

This means that we are obliged to read the Gospels in relationship to the rest of the New Testatment evidence. Hence the work of the apostolic band, as seen in the Pauline and Johannine literature, as well as in the record in Acts, must be taken into account here. There would seem to be no doubt that in this period of the Church's life, some representative principle such as we believe we have found in the Gospels themselves was present everywhere. It is likely that the Christian missionaries, as they travelled through the Graeco-Roman world, were compelled to set up some sort of "order" in the "churches" which they established.

In Jerusalem itself, we can be sure, such a pattern was soon laid down. And it is natural that this "order" was modelled on the Jewish customs and practice with which the earliest Jewish Christians were familiar. It is even *possible*, although not demonstrable, that Jesus Himself while carrying on His mission of preaching and teaching and healing and "casting out demons," had something like this pattern in mind when He called to him "the Twelve" and commissioned "the Seventy" to assist in the work for which He had been sent by the Father.

The position which was traditionally assigned to the Jewish elders and the institution of the Sanhedrin in a local synagogue, were already at hand for the early Christians. It was this kind of religio-societal "order" which the primitive community had known in their own experience. The local Jewish congregation, with its "board" of rulers, with the "council" which could act for the congregation in interpreting the Law and controlling the congregation's affairs, would provide a ready pattern. Hence it seems probable that in city after city, as the Gospel was preached and converts were won to the good news that Jesus was Messiah and that the "new age" was at hand because its powers had already been released in Him, something corresponding to a Sanhedrin, or council of elders, would be established to look after the affairs of each little flock of believers.

On the other hand, the Apostles themselves, as they travelled about on their mission, would very likely act in a general supervisory fashion. It is not too daring to say that what we would probably find in the primitive community is a Christian "presbyterate," in which the local "governors" act as a "council," doubtless with one of them serving as "president," while the travelling apostle, representing the whole Church rather than any particular cell within it, would carry on missionary work and act as bond of union of all believers. His function was to represent in this fashion the whole Church and the risen Lord of that Church, and so to serve as what one might well call "the steward" of the whole Church's faith and worship.

The Practice of the Primitive Christian Community

The years went on and the first apostles died. What then occurred? It is here that we are obliged to admit that degree of darkness concerning the course of events which led Salmon to speak of the "tunnel." But in the end, the various functions in the Church's life continued—whether it was by devolution, from the apostles, to certain functionaries chosen and ordained by them; or whether it was by evolution, from the presbyterate, of leaders who took over the particular functions which the apostles had carried on. There were general supervisors or what we may describe as "chief pastors"; there were members of local councils or governing bodies; and there were those who served in a diaconal capacity as "servants" of the Church, closely related to the supervisors. The attempt to demonstrate, either from Clement of Rome, or slightly later, from Ignatius of Antioch, that either the devolution or evolution theory of the rise of the full "three-ordered ministry" is to be accepted as proved on the level of sheer historical fact, would seem to have failed, for lack of conclusive evidence. And what evidence there is may be and has been interpreted in one way or the other, depending upon the presuppositions and predilections of the historian.

But we are not concerned with absolute demonstration. Neither are we interested in attempting to show that in some way or other the names given to various kinds of minister persisted along with the function which these ministers enjoyed. The functions themselves persisted, no matter what may have been the details of the development. That this is true is plain on the face of the evidence. The Church's order included, by the end of the "tunnel" period, a general ministry of supervision, a localized ministry of administration, and an auxiliary ministry of assistance. And the "succession" in the ministry of supervision may well be, as Dr. Arnold Ehrhardt has lately suggested (*The Apostolic Succession in the First Two Centuries of the Church*), a creation from Jewish-Christian sources based on succession lists of the Jewish high priests.

We can see, from as early as St. Ignatius of Antioch and from all later writers, that the head of the local Church was called the "bishop." We can see that the presbytery was still in existence, and it is clear that the diaconal office was maintained. It does not require any stretch of the imagination nor any special pleading to be equally certain that the continuing functions were filled by those who had been placed in them by some ceremony of the laying on of hands with appropriate prayers. Hippolytus, writing from Rome at a much later period (*circa* A.D. 217), makes this fact certain. For he reports a form which was used for ordinations, a form which is in essence Jewish and, excepting for specific Christian additions, is identical with that form which the experts tell us would have been used for the setting-apart of an elder in a Jewish Sanhedrin.

The Ministry That Emerged

From this complex background of Jewish and Christianized Jewish practice, we can see imaginatively the emergence of a ministry which carries on functions of a sacramental nature and which is itself representative in principle. And this is sufficient for our purpose, which is to show that, even apart from more detailed historical investigation of the primitive and early periods, with all their dubieties, the traditional ministry of the Church has a good claim to continue the functions which have been associated with the ordering of the Church from the beginning.

Now the actions which were assigned to the several ministers in those early days were carried on, not in any individualistic fashion, but on behalf of the Church as a whole. It was the work of the great Church. One cannot recall a single instance where claims were made for the *man* himself. Every reference to the ministry in the literature of the period is set in the context of the Church and its mission in the world. The bishop, who was understood by this time to be the symbol and guarantee of the Church's apostolicity—its *sent-ness* by Christ in and for the Church, in the power of the Holy Ghost—was the chief celebrant of the Eucharist which was the Church's "sacrificial" action.

He was the responsible officer in ordination on behalf of the Church. It was to him that appeal was made when the Church's faith was to be known and taught. But there is no suggestion that any of this was done by the bishop *apart from the Church;* his work was the work of the Church, or in more accurate phrasing, it was the work of Christ in His Church. The presbyters did not celebrate the Eucharist themselves; they assisted as co-celebrants seated round the bishop and thereby symbolizing the people of God. The deacons acted as the "bishop's men" both in the eucharistic rite, in almsgiving, and in many other respects, but they also were the servants of the Church.

This distribution of duties in the ministry was later modified, as need demanded. It was obviously impossible, when the membership in the Church had grown to immense proportions, for the bishop to celebrate at every Eucharist. Hence this function was usually delegated to the presbyters who acted for him; but in acting for him they were acting for Christ in His Church. This delegation and this representative functioning marked all their other duties. There is little doubt that we have at this point plain evidence of the devolution of function. There was a similar development in the work of the deacon, although his office continued for a much longer time to be the same as that of the early deacon.

It is certain that within, at most, one hundred and fifty years after the Resurrection, the normal ministry of the Church was that which we know as the ministry of bishops, presbyters, and deacons. While the particular distribution of duties changed as need grew, there is no reason to doubt that the symbol and the instrumental agent in the Church's unity, as in its apostolicity, was taken to be the bishop. And this, as we have noted, was before the faith of the Church had been worked out theologically, and before even eucharistic practice had become so precise.

Furthermore, it is noteworthy that once this norm had been established, the variations from it of which we have knowledge were few and unusual. Indeed, it is their exceptional character that brings them to our attention. For example, we hear of the fact that at Alexandria up to perhaps around A.D. 235—if St. Jerome's frequently cited account is to be trusted and his dislike of episcopal pretension has not affected his accuracy—the presbytery, or council of elders, elected and, by that fact and without further ordination, elevated their bishop. But this does no more than to indicate that in some places, or at least in this one place, there was deviation from what was or had become the normal usage. Even this exception, reported to us as part of St. Jerome's belligerent effort to minimize the episcopate and elevate the priesthood, did not long continue.

The Conclusion to Be Drawn

In the preceding pages we have attempted to give a summary account of what we think to be a possible and reasonable interpretation of the historical development of the ministry. But as we said at the outset, this is not to be taken as *proved*; it is to be taken as possible, as reasonable, even as probable. It is our contention that the "order" which we find at the close of the early period which we have discussed—say, roughly the third quarter of the second century—will give us a clue to the nature and function of the ministry in the Church. We see a Church order which stands sacramentally for Christ in His mystical Body. We see the emergence of a particular office which symbolizes and effects the continuity and the identity of the Christian tradition. We see the development from an earlier to a later representative ordering of the ministry, as particular functions are increasingly given to the presbyters in their several local churches. We see the diaconate carrying on its special work as the "servants of the Church" under the bishop.

And we should also recognize that the Church itself was regarded by this time, with a clarity which even the Scriptures themselves do not surpass, as a priestly society which embodied and continued the priestly work of the Lord himself. This means that the bishop's office and function was primarily to be "Chief Priest," which is, indeed, only another way of saying that he was "Chief Pastor," for Christ the Shepherd is Christ the great High Priest. This priestly idea was not simply an accident of history, nor was it an importation into non-sacerdotal Christianity from the Old Testament or from Gentile notions of priesthood. It was a profoundly Christian development to speak of the presbyters or elders of the Christian community, and above all of the bishop who was their overseer, as "priest." Indeed, as the Christian tradition developed its grasp of the meaning of its faith and worship, priesthood was seen as of the essence of the Church's life, and the Church's ministers were inevitably seen as exercising the function of ministering in priestly fashion on behalf of the priestly community. This function which originally centered in the bishop, but in which the presbyterate had shared as his corona, was a function which was now proper to the presbyterate itself, since it had been given over to them in response to the necessities of time and place.[1]

Summary

In conclusion, we must emphasize once more that if the Church be the Body of Christ, a truly organic and sacramental reality, it is legitimate to assume that it has observable "structures" whose intention is to maintain its historical continuity and to preserve its apostolic identity. In the last two chapters we have sought to describe these structures, providing for one of them—the ministerial articulation—an historical account of development from the first response made in faith to the impact of God in Christ. These "structures" are interrelated; they depend each one on the other. Hence a dismissal of the "Catholic faith" weakens the worship and life of the Church and sooner or later eviscerates the ministry of its traditional meaning. On the other hand, an overthrowing of the conception of the ministry in its more traditional sense may lead to serious changes in the nature of Christian worship, to alteration to the point of loss in the grasp of the specifically Christian life, and to reduction (or even, on occasion, denial) of the major assertions of the historic faith. The Church, we should insist, is "catholic" in this special sense; it is a richly integrated unity, in an organic and not merely an organizational or mechanical sense.

It is in some such fashion, we believe, that it may be maintained that the traditional Catholic ministry is necessary to the fullness of the Church. When the Anglican Ordinal declares that it intends that "these orders . . . be continued, and reverently used and esteemed," and when it affirms that "no man shall be accounted or taken to be a lawful Bishop, Priest, or Deacon," so far as the Anglican Communion is concerned, unless he "hath had Episcopal Consecration or Ordination," it is only saying that the One, Holy, Catholic, and Apostolic Church is a self-indentical organism, in which the very integrity of the Christian tradition is symbolized by a ministry which is "from the Apostles' time."

In the priestly Body of Christ, the ministry acts for the Lord, by His Spirit, in His Church. It would be historically anachronistic to attempt to go back to some conjectural ministry behind this one. It would be theologically unsound to deny the meaning which has been worked out for the ministry in the developing life of the Church, which the ministry symbolizes and which, in a sacramental fashion, it embodies. For the ministry is sacramental in two senses. It is a sacrament in that the actual service of ordination is performed by the use of material, physical, visible means, to effect an inward and spiritual grace. But it is sacramental in the further and much deeper sense that it stands for and expresses the interior reality of the Church itself. This is only another way of saying, that holy order stands for and expresses, within the context of the Body of Christ and as acting for that Body, Him who is the Lord and Head of the Church and of the whole race of men.

Dr. B. H. Streeter, in his study entitled *The Primitive Church,* remarked that episcopalianism, presbyterianism, and independency are all found in the earliest days of Christianity; hence, he said, "in the classic words of *Alice in Wonderland,* everyone has won and all shall have prizes." Unfortunately for Dr. Streeter, this is not in fact true. One particular ministry and not the others remained: that was "episcopalianism," if by this term is meant a ministry such as we have sketched in this chapter as integral to the Church in its full-fledged reality. The only "prizes" which the other types of ministry can be said to have received are "consolation-prizes"; for in the historical development of the Church they were not taken seriously until the Reformation, when certain of the reformers sought to return to the conjectural ministry which they felt they could recover from the New Testament and primitive practice. Our argument may have indicated why this does not prove their case.

IV

THE NATURE OF THE PRIESTHOOD

FOR ALL Christians, of whatever communion or denomination, there is one fact about the ministry which is indisputable and unshakeable. For us all, the one only essential and ultimate priesthood is the priesthood of our Lord Jesus Christ, incarnate, crucified, risen, and ascended, of Him in whom Very God dwelt in very man. This means in consequence that in any ultimate and entirely determinative sense there can be only one essential ministry in the Christian Church: the priesthood of Christ.

Here, we have said, is a fundamental assertion upon which all who profess and call themselves Christian must agree. Now, as we shall presently observe, this affirmation does not carry with it the corollary that it is improper to speak of priesthood in the Church's ordained ministry. Priesthood, in a derived yet genuine sense, may rightly be predicated of the ordained ministry of the Church. In fact we shall make it our major contention that precisely this must be done, if we are true to the historical view of the matter. But it is impossible to approach the problem of the ministry, and above all the question of the priesthood of the ordained minister, unless we are first quite clear that Jesus Christ alone is the source of all priesthood, because

He Himself *is* the Priest—"the great High Priest," as the New Testament calls Him.

Christ the High Priest

It is in the Epistle to the Hebrews, where this term appears, that the conception of the priesthood which all Christians ascribe to Christ is developed most fully, so far as New Testament material on the subject is concerned. There are many other passages where the same truth is indirectly asserted or implied; but it is in Hebrews that we find this teaching expressed explicitly and with singular clarity. It is natural that this should be so. The Epistle to the Hebrews is, from start to finish, a tractate concerned to defend Christianity, with its high claims for Jesus Christ, in terms of the ancient Jewish religion and the priestly and sacrificial practices of that religion. Although it is likely that the author of this document was profoundly influenced by Hellenistic—even by Platonizing—thought, his purpose was to use the accepted Jewish ideas as his background and to demonstrate the unique place of Christ by reference to those accepted ideas. Jesus is the fulfilment of all that the religion of the Hebrews asserted and did. The old Israel, after the flesh, had its priesthood, its Temple, its sacrifices. These, says the writer of this tractate, were by way of being intimation and adumbration of God's will and way for His people, and they had value for this reason.

But that God, who "at sundry times and in divers portions, spake in time past unto the fathers by the prophets, hath in these last days spoken unto us in a Son." The coming of Jesus is the coming of the Son, who is "heir of all things," the "brightness" of God's glory, "the express image of His Person." In Him, who "hath by inheritance obtained a more excellent name" even than the angels who serve God, God has "delivered them who through fear of death were all their lifetime subject to bondage"; and in Jesus, who "took on him not the nature of angels, but the seed of Abraham," we men have one who has been "made like unto his brethren, that he might be a merciful and faithful high priest in things pertaining to God, to make reconciliation for the sins of the people."

In His person, then, all that the ancient Jewish religion hinted and implied has reached its consummation and its fulfilment. He is the High Priest, who "when he had by himself purged our sins, sat down on the right hand of the Majesty on high." His death was the effectual sacrifice for sin, towards which complete sacrifice the ancient sacrificial rites in the Temple at Jerusalem were really pointing. He Himself in His human life with all that He did therein, was and remains "the new and living way" to the Father. The fullness of priesthood, sacrifice, reconciliation, are to be found summed up in Him.

The New Testament Witness

The entire New Testament witness agrees with this view. The picture which is presented to us is of One who is the Mediator between God and man, since He Himself is on both sides of whatever separates humanity from Deity. He is for *God* to man, and for *man* to God. As later theology was to put it, He is truly divine and truly human, yet one Person. Because such is the truth about Him, He can fulfil the priestly function of mediation between God and man; and He does this not by being a *tertium quid* which brings them together, but by uniting them in His own person, thus representing in His two natures (as the later theology would say) God to man and man to God.

This scriptural portrayal of the priesthood of Christ must be linked, moreover, with the interpretation of the meaning of the Church which is found in the New Testament and was then developed more fully in early and patristic thought. For St. Paul the Church, as we have seen, is related to Christ as Body to Head. For St. John Christ is the Vine, of which the members of the Church are the branches. In the exalted conception of the writer of the Epistle to the Ephesians, the Church and Christ together make a unity, Christ in and with His members. As a consequence of this kind of thinking, we may see that the true meaning of the term Christ, as Dr. Armitage Robinson pointed out long ago in commenting on Ephesians, is not the historic Jesus only, but Christ *and* His Church, Christ *in* His Church, Christ dwelling in and uniting Himself with those who are His. No later ecclesiastical teaching about the meaning of the Church has gone beyond this, nor would it be possible to hold a more exalted view.

The conclusion which may properly be drawn from this fact, when it is seen in relationship to the New Testament picture of Christ as High Priest, is that there is also a unique priesthood which appertains to the Church itself.

This priesthood of the Church, we may rightly say, is not simply an *extension* of the priesthood of the historic Jesus; it is in a real sense *identical* with the priesthood of Him who is both the historic Jesus and the risen Lord of Christian faith. For the New Testament Christ is one with His Church, which is His mystical Body. In saying this it also implies that that which appertains to Him must also appertain in some fashion to His Church. To speak of the priesthood of the Church as the people of God, "the royal priesthood" to which I Peter refers, is in fact to speak of the priesthood of Christ not (so to say) *in Himself* but *in His Body*. But since Christ, both in Himself and in His body, is one Christ, there is a profound truth in saying that the two priesthoods are in fact one.

An Objection Considered

The objection may be made that the Church, in its empirical representation in the world of history, can hardly be regarded as the perfect reflection of Christ Himself, the sinless Son of God who is the spotless Priest and Victim. The critic has a real point. The Church is, indeed, often in sin, prone to error, and weak in its hold on its Lord, on its faith in Him, and in loyalty to His divine purpose. Obviously these assertions are correct, and the objection must to that extent be allowed. But those who offer the objection with the avowed intention of minimizing the place of the Church or denying the fact of its divine reality, have convicted themselves of a view of the Church which is not to be found in the New Testament.

The Nature of the Priesthood

None of the writers of the New Testament would have been likely to disregard or to make light of the sin, error, and weakness of the Christian Church, as they met these things in the little communities with which they were in daily contact. We know that one of the main purposes of the Epistles, as well as of other parts of the New Testament and of much of the contemporary or near-contemporary literature of the Christian Church, was to correct error, to rebuke sin, and to fortify the Church wherever it might be planted. But at the same time, however, these early writers saw that there was more to the Church than met the eye.

Although it is obvious they did not and could not state their conception of the Church of the Body of Christ in the detailed language of later theology, they were in effect always affirming precisely that which the later theology affirmed. They were really saying that there is a sense in which the Church, like its Lord, is twofold in nature. As He is both divine and human, yet one; so the Church is the eternal, "supernatural" Body of Christ, "without spot or blemish," and yet at the same time is an empirical reality visible to men. Because its members are human, the Church in this empirical sense is open to the weaknesses of men and will manifest them in its corporate life. Those who expect that the empirical Church shall be entirely perfect have an inadequate understanding of the nature of the Church. They do what the New Testament writers never did; they overlook its human aspect, its historical conditioning. In doing this they forget that men and women, even when joined together in the company of the redeemed, are not made whole by some magical action which instantaneously removes their sinfulness and their shame. Even in the Church, men and women must grow in the grace which is implanted in them as they realize, actualize, fulfil—by God's empowering—what it means to be "very members incorporate" in Christ's mystical Body.

The Priesthood of All Believers

It is precisely through this incorporation into Christ, in His Body the Church, by the gracious and life-giving operation of the Holy Ghost, that all the members of the Church have their own share in Christ's priesthood. The New Testament again makes this clear, perhaps supremely in that document from which we have previously quoted, The First Epistle attributed to St. Peter. Primitive Christian thought on this priesthood of the laity was taken over and extensively developed by later Christian thinkers, who maintained that there was not only a priesthood which was Christ's in His Church, but that there was also a genuine priesthood which appertained to every member of the Church.

Thus we must affirm that all the members of the Church, "each in his vocation and ministry," are made sharers in the priesthood of Christ by their participation in His mystical Body. But they are not "priests" in their own right as men, nor are they "priests" by virtue of their own individual relationship to God. It is at this point that some of the reforming theologians, and in much more serious fashion certain of their successors, were led astray. Luther is usually cited on this point but not altogether fairly. He seems to have been clear enough on the matter which is here at issue. He erred, however, in assuming that because each Christian is a priest through participation in the priesthood of Christ, this must necessarily imply that all sacrificial functions as such have been done away because Christ Himself had performed on Calvary the great high priestly act for the whole Body. Luther does not appear to have recognized that the true meaning of the Church's eucharistic offering, which was the important question for him, is that it is neither the repetition nor the supplementation of the sacrifice of Christ, but that it is rather the Church's self-expression and its "pleading" of that sacrifice. In justice to Luther, however, it should always be said that late medieval thought had so degraded the Eucharist that it might, indeed, have seemed to many, if not to most, of the faithful to be a new or a supplementary sacrificial action; and in this respect Luther had the right on his side when he made his violent protest.

A Misinterpretation Answered

But there is no Christian ground for asserting, as some other theologians have done, that each Christian, standing in an individual relationship to God, can act "as his own priest." One has difficulty in seeing how any discerning Christian could ever accept or even envisage such a possibility, because he must know in the intimacy of his own experience that Jesus Christ alone is essential Priest. Whatever priestly function the Christian may humbly claim, this can be his only by participation. He can come to God, in a Christian sense, only through the "one Mediator and Advocate, Jesus Christ our Lord." He is "in Christ," which means that he is a member of the Body of Christ. Therefore he shares by grace, through the power of the Holy Spirit, in that which Christ by nature is; and he receives by faith, again through the power of the Holy Spirit, that which Christ has accomplished. This is evangelical and Catholic truth. Here is the scriptural and primitive view of the priesthood of all believers; this alone is the soundly Christian view of that priesthood. It is necessary to insist upon this point, and to say it over and over again, both against those who would forget the fact that God has in Christ made us "kings and priests," and also against those who would make the pretension that they can have an unmediated salvation. Sound theology and Christian life are at one in this matter.

The Doctrine of Priesthood Recapitulated

It may be convenient to summarize our argument thus far. The meaning of priest is "one who is representative of God to man and man to God"; a priest acts in the position of a mediator. But there is only one mediator between God and man, the Man Christ Jesus, as St. Paul is reported to have said. Hence Christ ultimately is the only Priest; in the fullest sense of ministry, His ministry is the only essential ministry in the Church. Yet because Christ is the Head and Life of the Church, which is His Body and hence is indissolubly united to Him, the Church shares in the very ministry and priesthood of Christ Himself. So we may properly speak of the Church as sharing Christ's "royal priesthood," and thus as His Body mediating between God and man, and representing God to man and man to God. This is the truth about the Church despite the sin, the error, and the weakness of the members of the Church on its empirical side. Distressing as these lapses must be to the faithful, who are however inextricably involved in them, the Church does manifest, empirically, the failures of men; yet the Church remains, by God's act and election, the Spouse and Bride of Christ. Its great responsibility is to *be itself*, empirically—that is, to realize and manifest in its historical existence that which is the divinely intended actuality of its nature in the purpose and will of God for His children. Finally, every Christian in fellowship with his brethren is a participant in the Church's priesthood which is Christ's own priesthood. This is the case because every Christian is by baptism made a member of Christ, which means that through baptism in water and by the Holy Spirit he becomes a participant in the life of the Body of Christ. Therefore he and all other believers with him have their part and place in Christ's mediatorial and representative action, which is the redemption of the world, precisely because they are His; as Christians they are branches in the Vine which is Christ Himself, living members of His mystical Body.

The Question of an Ordained Ministry

It is against this background in faith, just now briefly stated, that we may approach the question of the *ordained ministry* of the Church. The priestly quality which historic Christianity has consistently claimed for that ministry can be understood rightly and held in Christian terms on that one condition. If the considerations with which we have been concerned are forgotten, the *Christian* conception of the ordained minister's priesthood will be lost in a mass of pagan ideas—which alas! are not unknown in some quarters of the Christian world. The conclusion which must be drawn is that there is no Christian sense in which the ministry can be thought to impart its priesthood *to* the Church, nor is there any sense in which a Christian can think of the ministry as possessing a priesthood *apart from* the Church. Both of these notions are unscriptural and are the contradiction of essential Christian truth.

The priesthood—that is, the mediatorial and representative function—which is claimed in Catholic Christendom for the ordained ministry, is claimed as being received *from* the Church. For any theology which is adequately imbued with the Christian understanding of the Church and Christ's relationship to it, this can only mean that it is received from Christ, the Head, in and through his Spirit-filled Body. The ministry is the *Church's* ministry; it is, therefore, *Christ's* ministry in, and through, and for, and to, His church, within and by His Body.

We have noticed that it has sometimes been stated, or at

least the suggestion has been made, that the ministry has a separate line of descent from the historic Jesus and from the apostles, as it were outside of and apart from the Church. According to this view, there are evidently two lines which come down from the incarnate and crucified Lord. One is thought to be the line of community life, that of the Church; and the other to be the line of the ministry. Often, as in the teaching which the writer himself received as a youth, these two lines are described as if they developed side by side, with the ministry a kind of continuing pipe-line of priesthood, feeding into the Church the apostolicity which is claimed for it. Such a view has been implicit in the writings of some Roman theologians; often, indeed, it has been taught explicitly. It is not to be found among the Eastern Orthodox. In the Anglican tradition—excepting by some, in the Tractarian movement and its successor, the Oxford movement, influenced by what we can only de-scribe as a perversion of the New Testament and the primitive meaning of priesthood—it has never been held nor taught.

Even the better Roman theologies have hardly main-tained such a view. St. Thomas Aquinas, for example, does not seem really to have taught it. St. Thomas is without doubt the greatest systematizer of doctrine in western Christianity. His teaching, in a general sense, has become official in the Roman Catholic communion; and Christians of other communions can and should read him with respect as one of the greatest experts in traditional theology. Al-though St. Thomas did not develop his doctrine of the

Church or of the ministry in anything like the fullness with which many other doctrines were worked out by him, he is still sufficiently clear on this point, and it is amazing that the Roman Church does not appear officially to follow him here. We shall give one or two citations from his treatment of the ministry which are to the point.

St. Thomas writes, for example, that the priest consecrates the Eucharist "not by his own power, but as the minister of Christ, in whose person he consecrates" (*Summa Theologica*, III. 82.6). Again, he remarks that the priest says the words of the Eucharist "in the place of the entire Church, of which he is the minister" (S.T., III. 82.7). Elsewhere but in the same context, St. Thomas, discussing the priestly function, is ready to say explicitly that the ordained minister acts, not in his own right, but *in persona Christi*. Now Christ is Head of the Church, a theme which is developed at some considerable length in the section of the *Summa Theologica* preceding the treatment of the ministry, under the general discussion of the Incarnation. The priest acts "in the place of the entire Church." So, as acting *in persona Christi*, the priest is also acting *in persona ecclesiae*. Despite the powerful movement in his time towards a legalistic view of the Church and its ministry, Aquinas will not let himself fall into the error of separating that which is done *in persona Christi* from that which is done *in persona ecclesiae*. Thus, while he does not seem to teach the precise kind of relationship of Christ's priesthood and the Church's priestly nature with the priesthood of the minister which we have presented in the light of our study of the New Testament evidence, it is clear that he is moving in that direction. One may even think that he would have been prepared to make the assertion had the question been put to him in this form on the basis of the biblical material. It is hard to see how any responsible Christian theologian, conscious of the weight of New Testament material and the witness of the Fathers, could take a different position.

Summary

The argument which we have presented in this chapter ought not to suggest that the ordained ministry holds an unimportant place in the context of the Church's life. It is plain that the ministry is derived from, and is dependent upon, first Christ the High Priest and then the Church which is Christ's Body and shares in His priesthood. It is equally plain that the ministry is to be understood against the background of the "priesthood of all believers," which is theirs through participation in the Body of Christ. But neither of these considerations reduces for one moment the significance of the ordained ministry. Rather, each of them has its value in assisting us to put the necessity of the ordained ministry, with its priestly function, in the right context and to see it in the right perspective. There is all the difference in the world between saying that the only *essential* and *underived* priesthood known to Christians is that of Christ Himself, and saying that the ordained ministry does not possess anything which may properly be called by the name of priesthood. The two truths—Christ's originating priesthood and the sense in which priesthood may be ascribed to the ordained ministry—must be held in right proportion and balance. But both must be held, if we hope to be loyal to the general traditional position, which had its origin in the New Testament and was developed in the primitive Christian community.

In the next chapter we shall go on to discuss the theology of the ministry, as it grows out of the priesthood of Christ in His mystical Body the Church. We shall find that our best method for considering this will be to take as our guide the great work of Moberly, *Ministerial Priesthood,* published more than fifty years ago. We shall develop his line of argument and offer our own conclusions on the basis of his presentation; and we shall then proceed to a treatment of the particular sense in which the priesthood may be seen as not simply a "ministerial priesthood" for Christ's priesthood in the Church, but also (as Moberly himself would allow) a "sacrificing priesthood." This will necessitate our turning to the reply made in the late nineteenth century by the Archbishops of Canterbury and York to the papal encyclical which denounced Anglican orders; it will also necessitate our study of the more recent report of the Commission on Doctrine in the Church of England. In a succeeding chapter we shall give attention to the whole conception of the "historic episcopate" and its place in this context.

It is our conviction that the fundamental division between Catholic and Protestant views of the ministry is not centered so much in the episcopate itself as it is in the notion of priesthood. The episcopate becomes an obstacle to Christian reunion because it is the symbolic guarantee of the whole idea of a priestly, rather than a prophetic, ministry as normative in the Church. A priest can be ordained. A prophet cannot; he can only be recognized for what he is. But this means that the question of the *agent* in priestly ordination, and his function in the Church, is singularly important. It is, therefore, especially necessary that we give our attention to the last point. But since the idea of ministerial and sacrificing priesthood is one which presents the greatest difficulties to Protestant Christians as they seek to understand the historic ministry which the Catholic communions maintain and the claims which are made in the Catholic communions for that ministry, we are obliged to see the episcopate against that background of priesthood to which the present chapter has been devoted.

V

THE MINISTERIAL PRIESTHOOD

THE ordained ministry of the Church, since it fulfils priestly functions in and for Christ in His Body the Church, may appropriately be called a priesthood. But this priesthood which describes the function of the ordained ministry is always, and only, a ministerial priesthood. The phrase, ministerial priesthood, was used by R. C. Moberly in his study of the ministry, published under the same name, *Ministerial Priesthood*; that study is the most adequate treatment of the subject written by an Anglican theologian and is probably the most competent discussion of the ministry by any writer of any communion for several hundred years. Unhappily it is not much read nowadays; and this is the reason that much of the present chapter is devoted to the exposition of its major thesis.

Although details in historical statement and comments which depend upon points in biblical criticism are doubtless "dated" in Moberly's work, the main thesis is in our judgment so adequately presented and so satisfactorily defended that it still stands firm and sure. This thesis is that the ministry of the ordained man is a derived priesthood, a priesthood which comes from Christ in His mystical Body the Church, and which represents in a ministering fashion Christ in His Church. Thus it is also representative of, and ministers for, the priesthood of the divine society, a priesthood which all the faithful share by virtue of their membership in the Church, which means their sharing in the continuing incarnate and redeeming life of Christ Himself.

The Moberly Thesis on Priesthood

We shall begin by an exposition of Moberly's thesis. The reader may be referred to the book itself if he wishes to go into a more detailed presentation of the view which we are here accepting as basically sound. After this exposition, we shall proceed to a consideration of that aspect of ministerial priesthood which is particularly relevant to problems of reunion, namely the "sacrificing priesthood." This aspect of priesthood has been defined for Anglicans in a classical statement of the position of this communion —the reply of the Archbishops of Canterbury and York to the papal encyclical on Anglican orders. In that reply, the Archbishops sought to present a view of the nature of the ministry as a "sacrificing priesthood," which would not only meet the objections to Anglican orders brought forward by the Bishop of Rome, but would also have its basis in a sound, scriptural, and Catholic interpretation of the meaning of priesthood itself. We shall then look at material drawn from the report of the Commission on Doctrine in the Church of England, which states further the agreed

Anglican position on the ministry. We shall conclude by a consideration of the nature and function of the episcopate when seen in the context of this ministering priesthood of the Church.

It has been our contention that the Church as the Body of Christ shares in the priesthood which belongs to Christ its Head. Dr. Moberly gives a full statement of this contention; we quote him at length:

The sacrificial priesthood of the Church is really her identification with the priesthood and sacrifice of Christ. With this priesthood and sacrifice she is identified outwardly and inwardly; by outward enactment ceremonially, and by inwardness of spirit vitally. Christ himself has prescribed for all time an outward ceremonial, which is the symbolic counterpart in the Church on earth, not simply of Calvary, but of that eternal presentation of himself in heaven in which Calvary is vitally contained. Through this symbolic enactment, rightly understood—an enactment founded on and intrinsically implying as well as recalling Calvary—she in her eucharistic worship on earth is identified with his sacrificial self-oblation to the Father; she is transfigured up into the scene of the unceasing commemoration of his sacrifice in heaven; or the scene of his eternal offering in heaven is translated down to, and presented and realized in, the worship on earth . . . This identification of the Church on earth with the eternal presentation of the sacrifice in heaven, and with him who presents the sacrifice, means the reproduction in her of the Spirit of him who sacrificially offered himself. It is Christ who is being formed in her. It means therefore in her, as in him, the Spirit of Love which itself, in its outward expression on earth, is self-devoting sacrifice; or conversely, the spirit of sacrifice, of self-devotion, self-expenditure, which is, in the sphere of human life and duty,

the spontaneous and inevitable utterance of the Spirit of Love,
or of God.[1]

"All this," Dr. Moberly continues (*loc. cit.*), "is the in-
herent privilege of the members of the Body of Christ."
Christians share, therefore, in the priesthood of Christ because through their membership in Him they are members
also of His priestly life.

"What, then, is the priesthood of Christ's ordained ministers?" he goes on to ask. He answers the question in
these words:

The priesthood of the ministry follows as a corollary from
the priesthood of the Church. What the one is, the other is.
If the priesthood of the Church consists *ceremonially* in her
capacity of self-identification, through eucharistic worship, with
the eternal presentation of Christ's atoning sacrifice, and *spiritu-
ally* in her identification of inner life with the spirit of sacrifice
which is the spirit of love uttering itself in devoted ministry to
others, so it is by necessary consequence with the priesthood
of the ministry. For the priesthood of the ministry is nothing
distinct in kind from the priesthood of the Church.

The ordained priests are priestly only because it is the
Church's prerogative to be priestly; and because they are, by
ordination, specialized and empowered to exercise ministerially
and organically the prerogatives which are the prerogatives of
the Body as a whole. They have no greater right in the sacraments than the laity; but they, and not the laity, have been
authorized to stand before the congregation, and to represent
the congregation in the ministerial enactment of the sacraments which are the sacraments—and the life—of both
alike . . .

We [cannot] draw an essential contrast between the priesthood of the Church and of the ministry. The powers, the privileges, the capacities, are the powers and privileges and capacities of the body as a whole.

Yet this is not the whole story. For, as Moberly says,

We utter protest against the unauthorized *sequitur* which would conclude that therefore the powers of the whole can be ministerially exercised by any, or by all. It is not given to the eye to hear, nor to the ear to see. Those who actually celebrate do but organically represent, and act for, the whole. But the executive right, the power to represent, and act for, and wield ministerially the capacities of the whole, is not indiscriminate. Those who stand before the congregation, either as its representative organs to Godward, or as the accredited ministers of God to it, must be authorized and empowered to do this. We shall I believe approach the truth in this matter, neither on the one hand by exalting the ministry at the expense of the laity, nor on the other—and even less—by dropping the distinctive words priestly and priesthood; but by insisting, in no metaphorical sense, upon the sacred character and the solemn responsibility of the priesthood of the Christian Church as a whole, and (apart from its ministerial and executive sense) of every individual lay-member of the Church.

This is the essentially necessary background for any consideration of the ordained ministry. Moberly now proceeds to discuss the meaning of the priesthood which may be ascribed to ordained ministers. He writes:

They are priests because they are personally consecrated to be the representatives and active organs of the priesthood of the Church. And they represent it emphatically in both of its directions. In the ceremonial direction they represent it as divinely empowered to be themselves its leaders and instruments. And from this representative leadership in all external enactment of worship and sacrament . . . it follows also, on the inward and spiritual side, that those who outwardly represent the priesthood of the Church must no less specially represent it in its true inwardness.

That means, he tells us, that the minister

cannot but be a representative *persona*. He is always, in his own spiritual attitude and effort—to Godward for man, to manward for God—called to realize, and (as it were) to personify, the characteristic priestliness of the Church. This is not because he is an intermediary between Christ and his Church; it is not because he is something which the Church is not; but because he is set to represent, in his own personality, with an eminent distinctiveness, that which the whole Church cannot but essentially be . . . This priestly spirit . . . is *not* the exclusive possession of the ordained ministry; it is the spirit of the priestly Church. But those who are ordained "priests" are bound to be eminently leaders and representatives of this priestliness of spirit, and they have assigned to them an external sphere and professional duties which constitute a special opportunity, and a charisma of grace which constitutes a special call and a special capacity, for its exercise.

The conclusion of the matter is put by Moberly in these words:

It is necessary, then, to emphasize unreservedly the truth that the priesthood of ministry and of laity are not really antithetical or inconsistent, but rather correlative, complementary, nay, mutually indispensable ideas. Magnify first the solemnity of ministerial priesthood, and then from that expound the dignity and power of the priesthood of the laity; or, if you will, magnify lay priesthood first, and mount from thence to its concentrated meaning in those who are set apart personally to represent the collective priesthood, and to wield it ministerially (*op. cit.* pages 257-262, *passim*).

It is worth noting, incidentally, that St. Thomas Aquinas likewise takes this "ministerial view." In commenting on absolution pronounced by a priest, he says that while "God alone absolves from sin and forgives sin absolutely, yet priests do both *ministerially*" (*Summa Theologica.*, III. 84.3, resp. ad obj. 3). With this should be linked our remarks on St. Thomas's views of priesthood, quoted earlier in this book.

Moberly's Thesis on the Episcopate

Reference should be made here to Moberly's view of the nature of the episcopate, as it is related to the concept of the ministerial priesthood. The preface to the second edition of his work provides a useful summary of his position. The episcopate, he writes, is indeed marked by growth, but its "connection, in principle, with apostolate is too vital in character; its existence is at once too early and too widespread, not only as a form of Christian ministry, but as the symbol of Church unity and authority, and therefore as a foundation essential for the legitimacy, and for the due transmission, of all other ministries and sacraments in the Church," for it to be dismissed "as a mere example of not illegitimate evolution." On the contrary, he says, there was "a principle of which 'commission' was the essence," and the apostolic ministry became "as the immediate outcome of the first half-century of Christian experience, and therefore of the apostolic work as a whole, the one orderly mode and guarantee."

Dr. Moberly then observes, of his argument as here given:

It is not contended that either apostolic transmission, or anything which can fairly be regarded as episcopacy, were thus recognized as universal or necessary conceptions in the first exuberant flush of the Church's pentecostal experience. It is not denied that the channels which existed from the first, and were to be more and more explicitly recognized as the channels divinely appointed for indispensable order, were at first too freely and too richly overflowed to be formally distinguishable as channels.

Yet it is plain that such channels were at length seen to be "the indispensable conditions of a system of order guaranteed and continuous, throughout the life of a great historical community" (p. xxiv-xxvi, *passim*).

There was certainly "natural development," but "from the time and as the outcome of the translation of the divine principle of ministry into living action through the working of the Spirit in the apostolic age as a whole . . . episcopacy stands forth, not as a novel, still less as a merely accidental growth, but as original, fundamental, and essential to the unity, continuity, and spiritual security of the Church" (p. xxviii).

No one can read the quotations which we have given nor follow the line of argument in Moberly's study, without recognizing that here is a conception of the nature of ministry which safeguards the truths that were reasserted at the time of the Reformation against perversions and errors that had grown up in the western Church, while at the same time it is loyal to that understanding of the ministry which has been held within Catholic communions from early days. But we must go on from there, because the priesthood which we have seen to be thus "ministerial" is also, as Moberly himself has intimated, to be seen as in a real sense a "sacrificing priesthood."

A Sacrificing Priesthood

What does this idea of "sacrificing priesthood" involve? If we seek to state this without refinements of theory, we can say that it means that the minister is one who as a central part of his office "offers sacrifice." The ministerial priest does this since he acts for Christ in His Church, and in thus acting for Christ in His Church he officiates at the Eucharist, which is described in the communion office of Anglican Prayer Books as "the sacrifice of praise and thanksgiving." It is, of course, clear that a conception of sacrifice might conceivably carry with it a whole collection of ideas, either Jewish in origin or derived from pagan cults or the ethnic religions, which would be alien to the Christian view of the relation of God and man and thus might be the negation of the Christian Gospel which proclaims the means of reconciliation between God and man.

But this is not necessarily the case, and Anglican formularies are designed to state a different view. To discover what, in Anglican thought, is the soundly scriptural and the authentically Catholic view of the Christian ministry in this regard, we may turn to the Reply which was made in 1897, by the Archbishops of Canterbury and York, to the bull of Pope Leo XIII, published in 1896. In that bull the Pope declared that for the Roman Church the orders of the ministers of the Anglican Communion are invalid, since Anglican ordinations are not, in the view of Roman theologians, intended to make priests who can offer sacrifice.

We are not here concerned with the question of the "validity" or "invalidity" of Anglican orders, although the reply of the Archbishops demonstrated their technical validity and also showed that the Roman pontiff and his advisors were in error in important matters of fact and mistaken in significant matters of theology. Our interest is in the conception of the priesthood, especially in its "sacrificing" function, which was enunciated by the Archbishops in the course of their Reply. We turn to the document itself for clarification of this point.

The Statement of Canterbury and York

First of all, the Archbishops show that the Anglican Church, at the time of the Reformation, had no intention of departing from the traditional ministry of the historic Catholic Church. Indeed, as they demonstrate, the intention of the Reformers in England was explicitly stated as the maintenance of that ministry. The title and preface of the Ordinal, to which we have already drawn attention, are cited to show that "the succession and continuance

of these offices"—that is, bishop, priest, and deacon—
"from the Lord through the Apostles and the other ministers of the primitive Church is . . . clearly implied."

Not only does this appear from the title and preface
of the Ordinal itself, but in the Ordinal text, in "the
'eucharistical' prayers which precede the words, *"Receive
the Holy Ghost,"* the intention is made equally plain. The
purpose which animated those who drew up the Ordinal
was not only "to keep and continue these offices which
come down from the earliest times," but it was also to use
and esteem them "in the sense . . . in which they were
received from the Apostles and had been in use up to
that [the Reformers'] time." The Archbishops go on to
say that contrary to the papal claim, it is not simply a
theory entertained by "a newly formed party" in the
Anglican Communion, but the "intention of our Church"—
that is to say, of the whole tradition and spirit of the Anglican Reformation—that this should be so (pp. 58-60).

What the Archbishops call (p. 58) "the character of the
priesthood," includes "the ministry of more than one
mystery." The meaning of the Christian ministry can be
demonstrated in what the Pope in his bull had called "the
necessary connection between faith and worship, between
the *law of believing and the law of praying.*" At this point
the Archbishops indulge in a bit of argument which is
peculiarly relevant to our discussion. For the Roman Mass
itself is described by the Archbishops as agreeing "sufficiently with our [Anglican] eucharistic formularies," since
the words of that office show that it is indeed a sacrifice,

offered by the priest, a sacrifice which is portrayed in "four ways."

"Firstly it is a 'sacrifice of praise.' " In the second place, "it is the offering made by God's servants and His whole family, about which offering request is made that it 'may become to us the Body and Blood' of His Son our Lord." Thirdly, "it is an offering to His Majesty of His own 'gifts and works.' " And finally, in the Roman rite, it is a sacrifice "compared with the sacrifices of the patriarchs . . . and with that offered by Melchisedech," which is a sacrifice "not only of the offerer, but also of the things offered."

The phrases about the patriarchs and Melchisedech are of course not in the Anglican eucharistic rites, but the relationship of the Christian Eucharist with the oblation of the Old Testament worthies is implicit in the whole action as found in Anglican rites, which, therefore, parallel the teaching suggested by the Roman rite itself. The Archbishops are careful to point out, however, that later Roman *teaching,* as at the Council of Trent, has contradicted what the rite itself suggests. In conclusion the Archbishops declare that for all historical Christian thinking, and for Anglican theology, "the sacrifice of the eternal Priest and the sacrifice of the Church . . . in some way certainly are one"; but they reverently decline to enter into "subtle disputations" or "too precise definitions," preferring to regard the eucharistic sacrifice as "full of mystery," "to be treated with the highest reverence," which is to be considered always not as a subject for disputation but as "a bond of Christian charity" (p. 36-37).

It is against this background that the Archbishops outline the function of the priest, in the whole eucharistic action as the Anglican tradition understands it. "The eucharistic sacrifice," they affirm, is one "in which the people has necessarily to take its part with the priest." The actual celebration is, of course, committed "only to properly ordained priests and to no other ministers of the Church." But it is the Anglican position, the Archbishops assert, that the Eucharist which these ordained priests "celebrate is no nude commemoration of the sacrifice of the Cross." It is a genuine sacrifice. There follows in the Reply a description of this sacrificial action, as the Church of England performs it in its eucharistic office:

In the Liturgy which we use in celebrating the holy Eucharist,—while lifting up our hearts to the Lord, and when now consecrating the gifts already offered that they may become to us the Body and Blood of our Lord Jesus Christ— [we] signify the sacrifice which is offered . . . in such terms as these: We continue a perpetual memory of the precious death of Christ, who is our Advocate with the Father and the propitiation for our sins, according to His precept, until His coming again. For first we offer the sacrifice of praise and thanksgiving; then next we plead and represent before the Father the sacrifice of the Cross, and by it we confidently entreat remission of sins and all other benefits of the Lord's Passion for all the whole Church; and lastly we offer the sacrifice of ourselves to the Creator of all things, which we have already signified by the oblations of His creatures.

This total action, the Archbishops say, "we are accustomed to call the eucharistic sacrifice."

From this evidence, presented by the highest Anglican authority, we can see that there can be no doubt that the priesthood of the Anglican Church is continuous with the historic priesthood of the Church and is ordained, among other things, for the offering of a sacrifice in which the people, too, have their place. There can be no doubt, either, that it is basic Anglican teaching that the bishops of the "Reformed" Church of England and of the Anglican Communion as a whole are by the intention of that Church, and through the safeguarding of the usual line of succession in consecration to the episcopate, continuous with the historic episcopal office of the Catholic Church. We shall return to this point in the next chapter. It will suffice to say here that the Anglican Communion has officially defended a ministry which is priestly in character and ordained to continue the function of offering, on behalf of the Church of Christ, the perpetual memorial of the Passion of Christ.

The Statement of the Commission on Doctrine

The *Report of the Commission on Doctrine in the Church of England,* published in 1938 after many years of study and conference, sums up and states the agreed position of various schools of thought in the Church of England, indicating divergences where these occur. It carries on the same general line regarding the ministry which we have noted in Moberly's book and in the Archbishops' Reply. The discussion of the ministry (found on pages 114-124 of the published Report) is of interest to us because it introduces the concept of the episcopate. A brief summary of the section will be of value for our argument.

"The fundamental Christian ministry," says the document, "is the ministry of Christ. There is no Christian priesthood or ministry apart from His." This affirmation, which is of course in agreement with our own insistence throughout this book, leads the commissioners to the further statement that "the Church as the Body of Christ, sharing His life, has a ministerial function derived from that of Christ." The "recognized focus and organ of authority, the Apostolate," is said to be "an original element, but not the sole constitutive element, in the life of the Church," as the New Testament presents the picture. After a warning lest later "formality" be read back into the primitive Church, the Report says that "the ministry does not exist apart from the Body, nor the Body apart from the ministry." "But Christ, in drawing men to Himself, unites them in a fellowship of which the Apostolate, which He appointed, and the ministry, which is its successor, are the ministerial organs."

The document gives a survey of the development in "form" of the ministry with special reference to the preservation of continuity in the Church's "ministerial organ." It then affirms,

We cannot accept a conception of ordination which is exclusively hierarchical, as though the ministerial succession

alone constituted the essence of the Church apart from any
continuing body of the faithful; or, on the other hand, a conception which would make the ministry representative only
of the congregation, or of the whole body of the laity, or again,
a conception which regards it as having its justification only
in administrative convenience. The ministry is to be regarded
as having its entire existence and significance within the life
of the Body as a whole. The fact that the ministry does not
derive its commission from a Church which initially had no
ministry, but derives it, within the Church, from Christ Himself, the Head of the Church, His Body, does not involve the
consequence that it can perform its functions apart from the
Body. Continuity of ministerial succession, though it is the
pledge of unity and continuity in the sphere of order, is not the
only pledge of unity and continuity of the Church's life.[2]

We may recall here the insistence, in earlier chapters
of this study, that it is precisely because the ministry is
one of the "structures" of the Church, although not the
only one, that it can be conceived as a necessary articulation in the response of the community of faith to the impact of God in Christ. This is what gives it a peculiar
function and meaning in the life of the Body of Christ.
The faith of the Church, the eucharistic worship of the
fellowship and the persisting life-in-grace, are together with
ministry or holy order the Church's pledge of "unity and
continuity," not the ministry apart from the faith, worship,
and life, but rather the ministry as included with and
standing for those other articulations.

In its treatment of the episcopate, the Report is insistent

on the double truth that while "we do not doubt that God has accepted and used other ministries which through breach of continuity in the past are deficient in outward authorization," it is also the fact that "the Anglican Communion has been right to regard the historic episcopate as in a special sense the organ of unity and continuity." The several arguments which have traditionally been adduced for the episcopate are then briefly stated, reaching their conclusion in the assertion that the episcopal office is "the appropriate agent for carrying on through ordination the authority of the apostolic mission of the Church." The reason for this, it is said, is that the episcopate may be seen to have become historically "the organ of this mission and authority," "to guard the Church against erroneous teaching," by acting as the "living representative of the unity and universality of the Church." Thus the bishop is "Chief Pastor," who in this capacity "represents in a special degree the paternal quality of pastoral care."

The *purpose* of the ministry is said to be that it shall "express and mediate," through official and ritual functions, "the life of Christ in His Body, alike in worship offered to the Father and in ministry to the needs of men." But it is to do this in a functional fashion, "holding commission to act in the name of the whole Church." And in the view of the Commission the episcopate is the proper agent to secure that the ministry shall be so commissioned: it is "the appropriate" organ for the particular function of securing such "unity and continuity."

We need not repeat the discussion of the priesthood

The Ministerial Priesthood

(p. 156-159 of the published Report), for it parallels in essential theological structure and often in detail the views which have been presented earlier in this chapter, especially in the discussion of the subject by Dr. Moberly.

VI

THE EPISCOPATE

———

WE NOW TURN to the episcopate in the life of the Church. What is the function and place of the episcopate in the priestly ministry of the Church? An immediate answer is given in one Anglican formulary. The office of a Bishop, says the American Book of Common Prayer in its Offices of Instruction (page 294), is "to be a chief pastor in the Church; to confer Holy Orders; and to administer Confirmation." Or, in the language we have used earlier, the bishop is that minister in the priestly Body of Christ who stands for, symbolizes, and effectually represents the apostolic faith, the apostolic worship, and the apostolic life-in-grace. As such he is the chief "steward of the mysteries of Christ."

When we look back into the early history of the Christian community, we can see that the continuity of the Church was indeed safeguarded by the episcopal office. For our present purpose it is irrelevant whether this was at first continuity or succession in the see (as presumably in St. Irenaeus) or, as was later also the case, succession in a line of ordination or consecration. The New Testament scriptures were the "proof" of the Gospel and of the sacraments; but the bishop, who held office as "successor to the apostles," was the guardian of the Scriptures, the teacher of the faith, and the chief minister of the sacraments. He ordained and consecrated the clergy; he was the supervisor of the flock in the city or area for which he had been commissioned. In the main, he was also responsible for the "government" of the Church, but it is important to note that this was not his *essential* function. Indeed, in primitive days, much if not most of the "government" was apparently in the hands of the council of presbyters, over which, doubtless, the bishop presided but which as a group directed the Church in its affairs. Later the full "monarchical" episcopate was normal in the Church and the bishop then assumed the sole governing power; but it was still possible, centuries afterward, to have a situation such as that which prevailed in the early days of the Church of Ireland, where the monasteries with their abbots exercised government over the Church, while the bishops retained as their peculiar function the stewardship of the sacraments and the ordination of the clergy.

The Development of the Episcopal Office

The episcopate has indeed developed in such a fashion that government of the Church has seemed, especially in Anglican polity, to be its principal function. Yet its chief and characteristic *spiritual* function remains what it always was. The bishops are the guardians and symbols of the Church's historic continuity and of its self-identity in faith and worship. This means, of course, that it is impossible to speak of the historic episcopate without attaching to it some definite meaning. There must be a "theory" concerning the nature and function of the episcopate, and it is absurd to pretend that it is possible to have bishops without any reason for having them. To do this would be to put the episcopate in the same category as fetishes and other superstitions and magical devices. But the "theory" of the episcopate, involving as it does the idea of some genuine "succession," need not be the oft-held Tractarian view which, as we have seen, erroneously holds that the episcopate "makes" the Church.

The normative Anglican theory as to the historic significance of the episcopate, as both Moberly and the *Doctrinal Report* make clear, is that it has been the means by which the Church, which is the Body of Christ, symbolizes and maintains a visible historical continuity and a visibly persisting identity in its life and work. This does not imply that there can be no Church without a bishop, but rather that the fulness of the Church's life includes the episcopate as symbol and sign of its true continuity and identity. The way in which this has been accomplished historically is by the "laying on of hands" upon those called to the sacred ministry by one who is a functional representative of the Church's apostolicity which is Christ's apostolicity. This method of symbolizing the apostolic ministry has carried with it the corollary that the bishop is himself the chief minister of the Church, under Christ. The bishop's office is given significance in that it is the instrumental means by which visible apostolicity is symbolized, although in the very fact of its being such a symbol it is representative of the one ultimate essential ministry of Christ for which it is the organ.

It has been the contention of the Catholic communions that ordination by a bishop, himself rightly consecrated, effectually authenticates a given man as the duly accredited agent of the whole Church in each and every function which may pertain to his ministerial office. This is the only meaning which can properly be attached to the word "validity." "Validity" is a term which might well be given up, since it seems almost invariably to suggest erroneous ideas both to those who use it favourably and to those who dislike it. If it *is* employed, however, it is always to be used in respect to such historical authentication; it has nothing to do with the blessing which unquestionably is given, and always has been given, by God to those who would serve Him, not least when they are seeking to do this through non-episcopal ministries. This is a point which we must consider in more detail in a later chapter.

The Meaning of Apostolic Succession

Furthermore, as Dr. E. L. Mascall has rightly remarked in an essay appearing in *Theology* (June 1949), "the real point of apostolic succession is not" (and here we should interpolate, in the interest of theological adequacy, the adverb "only") "that it gives the Church militant of today continuity with the Church militant of the past, but that it gives continuity with the Church expectant and triumphant today." It is important that the doctrine of the unity of the Church in a vertical as well as horizontal direction be central to our thinking about the ministry. Much discussion of the ministry, like much discussion of the Church, is entirely on the horizontal line. Continuity in time and space are regarded as essential, but the eternal reality of the Body of Christ, in its divine fulness, is not seen as involved equally with the historical reality with which the empirical Church confronts us. The fact is that "unless we discuss the theology of the ministry and the apostolate," to continue from Dr. Mascall, "in ontological and eschatological terms, our understanding of them will be totally inadequate." It is for this reason that we must assert the ontological status of the ministry of the Church, in relation to the Church as being itself an ontological reality; and it is with this thought in mind that we must also insist upon the unity which exists between the Church as we know it in its empirical, this-worldly manifestation and the Church in its eschatological aspect—that is, the Church as the actual Body of Christ, "without spot or wrinkle," fulfilling the divine purpose and including in its membership the saints and holy ones, the souls of those who are now dead but are by anticipation in their true *patria,* and those who now as pilgrims are *in via* as members of the Church militant here in earth.

The bishop symbolizes the whole Church and in ordaining authenticates for the whole Church, in its *whole* reality. He represents the whole Christ, *totus Christus caput et corpus.* All of this is involved when we speak of the "apostolic succession" in any proper meaning of that misused phrase—the authorizing and empowering of men to act in the ministerial priesthood, either as chief pastors or in the other orders which receive their authorization at their hands.

The Church's *government,* so far as administrative and executive activities are concerned, could from this point of view just as well represent the merging of episcopal, presbyterian, congregational, and other types of "polity." Indeed, in the American branch of the Anglican Communion, something of this sort has been accomplished, with the government of the Church in the hands of the General Convention and its two houses, the diocesan conventions, and the standing committees in each diocese. There is no reason that such a procedure should not be followed more generally, and an increasingly "democratic" constitution, administratively speaking, be developed in communions that hold to episcopal order. This should be made quite clear in all reunion discussions. The bishop is properly to be regarded neither as an elected officer in a business administration nor as a mere figurehead, any more than he is to be seen as a feudal prince or a Hanoverian prelate. He is one who fulfils the traditional and symbolic function of "Father in God." This is the primitive Catholic view, which makes impossible both prelatical claims and fancy episcopal pretensions. These have nothing to do with the office. They are indeed a perversion of that office; and although they may well be understandable in the light of historical circumstance, they are in no sense implicit in the nature of the episcopate itself.

The Episcopate in the Context of Ministerial Priesthood

The episcopate can only rightly be understood when it is set in the context of the ministerial priesthood of the Church. For the significance of the bishop's office is that he is "chief priest," functioning in and for the Body of Christ, acting for the Church as the steward of its faith and sacraments, as the agent in its ordinations, and as the overseer of its flock. His work, so to say, is both a vitalizing and a pastoral work. He does in fact govern, but this government is essentially in the realm of spiritual affairs, however many responsibilities of another sort may from time to time have been given to him through the exigencies of the historical situation. Such a conception of the episcopal office, which relates it directly and meaningfully to the ministerial priesthood and thus to the Church's priesthood in Christ, puts it in the right perspective and has its profound relevance to the real points at issue in reunion discussions. It is for this reason that our emphasis has been upon this side of the ministry, rather than upon the specific duties and the detailed responsibilities which have developed through the centuries and have devolved upon those holding the office of bishop in the Church of God.

We have maintained that the only essential ministry in the Church is that of Christ Himself. All other ministry is derivative, although it is in a secondary sense necessary to the Church. Christ's ministry—above all His priesthood —is the essential reality of the Church's inner life. As Christ is the great High Priest, so the Church which is His mystical Body is possessed of priesthood. Every member of the Church, by virtue of his participation in the life of Christ, shares in the priesthood of the laity, which is the priesthood of the people of God. The ordained ministry, functioning always on behalf of and for the Body of Christ, functions thereby in a ministerial fashion for Christ as Priest, for Christ as Priest in His priestly Church. George Tyrrell once expressed this conception in fine words: "The priest is but the authenticated instrument and representative through whom the whole Church functions, and it is Christ, or the Church, who baptizes, blesses, consecrates, anoints, absolves, teaches, and rules" (*Scylla and Charybdis*, p. 50).

The corollary of this is that the ministry of the ordained man is not something which belongs to him as an individual right; it is always functional and representative. This is what gives to the ordained man the particular *character* or stamp, as classical theology has put it, which sets him indelibly apart as the ministering agent of the risen Lord in His Body, by the operation of the Holy Spirit. No priest can rightly speak of "his" sacrament, nor say that he is celebrating "his" Eucharist. No bishop ordains in his own name or by his own right. In every instance of ministerial action, the bishop or the priest is acting as the agent and representative of Christ in His Body; he is *in persona ecclesiae* and therefore *in persona Christi*. So all prelacy, all sacerdotalism, and all priestly pretension, are done away; humility is the only possible attitude for one who is called to this high office in and for the Church and its Lord. "Not that we lord it over your faith, but that we are the helpers of your joy."

The Orders in Ministry

Yet the ordained ministry, in all its levels, is different from what we loosely and inaccurately call the laity. It is different simply in that it has been given its own peculiar "vocation" in the life and work of the Church. The bishop is set apart to be chief pastor and chief priest, and to ordain. The priest—and, of course, the bishop too—is set apart to act as the Church's agent in presenting "the continual remembrance of the sacrifice of the death of Christ," to preach the Gospel, to absolve and to bless, in the Lord's name and as the Lord's representative. The deacon is set apart to be a ministering assistant, under the bishop and for the people of God. But all of these are "vocations," each with its special functions, within the context of the life of the Church which is Christ's.

The best illustration of what is meant by this teaching about diversity of function in the Church of Christ may be seen in the characteristic Christian action, the Eucharist itself, for here we have the faithful gathered in a given place and focussing at a point the whole Church. Let us picture an occasion when the bishop is in a parish for his visitation and is celebrating the Eucharist for the flock of Christ.

The people are present at the service "to assist," as the old phrase has it, in the eucharistic offering. They have their necessary duties and their proper responsibilities. Of these duties and responsibilities their responses to the prayers and above all their saying of the *Amen* stand as the great symbol. In the sanctuary are the special assistants at the service: the acolytes who represent the laity in the actual conduct of the service and in the preparation of the elements of bread and wine, and the choir which sings the service. The ordained ministers are engaged in the celebration. There may be an epistoler and a gospeler, each with his special duties. There is the celebrant himself, on this occasion the bishop, who says the words and performs the actions which are required for the right fulfilment of Christ's command, "Do this in remembrance of me." Angels and archangels are there, with "all the company of heaven," including the saints and holy ones who now stand at God's throne. In its prayers the Church remembers and pleads before God for all those who have kept the faith and now rest in peace, awaiting their final consummation in God's heavenly kingdom. The material and physical world, and man's labours in it, are represented in the elements which are to become the spiritual food of the Body and Blood of Christ. They also, in their way, are "of the Church," for they are the earnest of the whole redeemed cosmos, when Christ shall deliver the kingdom to the Father that God may be all in all.

One Priesthood

Now none of those who are present at the Eucharist can be said to be more *important* than the others. The Eucharist cannot be offered unless there is a congregation; and the action of the ministering priest—in this particular instance a bishop, but more often one who has been ordained by him on behalf of the Church—is necessary if the sacrament is to be celebrated. There are, indeed, differences in function, but all who are present at the service are one in the great eucharistic action. The claim which can be made uniquely for the bishop, or for the priest who has been ordained by a bishop to the priestly ministry, is precisely that he has been set apart, by consecration or ordination, for this very thing. He is to perform, and if a bishop to ordain others to perform, on behalf of the Church and as acting for Christ in His Church, that which our Saviour directed should be done. That is all; and that is enough.

The late Archbishop of Canterbury, William Temple, summed it up in an address which has been reprinted in a collection of his occasional speeches:

When we go back to the first records of the Church we find neither a ministry which called people into association with it, nor an undifferentiated fellowship which delegated powers to a ministry; but we find a complete Church, with the apostolate accepted as the focus of administration and authority. When the Lord's earthly ministry was ended, there was found in the world as its fruit and as means of continuance this Body, in which the distinction of ministry and laity is already established. The apostles were in no sense ministers of the laity; they were ministers of Christ to the laity, and to the world waiting to be won. They took steps for the perpetuation of the ministry, and it has descended to ourselves. So when I consecrate a godly and well-learned man to the office and work of a bishop in the Church of God, I do not act as a representative of the Church, if by that is meant the whole number of contemporary Christians; but I do act as the ministerial instrument of Christ in His Body the Church. The authority by which I act is His, transmitted to me through His apostles and those to whom they committed it; I hold it neither from the Church nor apart from the Church; but from Christ in the Church . . .

This authority to consecrate and ordain is itself witness to the continuity of the life of the Church with its unceasing dependence on its Head, Jesus Christ, who is the same yesterday and today and forever. Every priest who by virtue of his ordination celebrates the Holy Communion acts not for the congregation there present, not for all Christian people then living on the earth, but as the organ of the Body of Christ, the ministerial instrument of Christ active in and through His Body; so that though no more than two or three persons be actually assembled, yet the congregation at that Holy Communion service is the communion of saints, with which the persons present, be they few or many, are there conjoined . . .

It is possible to hold such a faith without the sacramental expression of it in the apostolic ministry; but those who by God's election have received that ministry will neither surrender it nor so hold it as to make difficult the access of others to it. We hold it as a treasure and a trust. It is our duty both to safeguard it and to commend it, both to preserve it for ourselves and our children, and to make easy the way of entering into participation in it, provided only that in making our treasure available we do not dissipate or squander it.[1]

Here is a noble statement of the significance of the ministry, "as this Church hath received the same," which is at once firm in its insistence on the truth of "holy order" historically received, but also generous in its spirit towards those who do not possess that particular gift. The Christian Church is the fellowship of whose continuity and identity "the ministry of apostolic succession" is both a symbol and an expression. As some recent writers have well said, it is not of the *esse* of the Church, since there could be a Church without it; it is not only of the *bene esse* of the Church, since this introduces futile argumentation about the meaning of "well-being"; it *is* of the *plene esse* of the Church, because it is part of the fulness of the Christian tradition, the token of our fellowship with all the faithful, living and departed, and the symbol of the continuity of the Body of Christ now with Him, who lived and died for us and who ever liveth to make intercession for us.[2]

VII

THE HISTORICAL MINISTRY AND
THE PROBLEM OF CHRISTIAN REUNION

———

A CAREFUL EXPLORATION of the questions having to do with the nature of the Church and the meaning and function of the Christian ministry is of first importance in all approaches to the reunion of a divider Christendom. Unfortunately it is not always recognized that this is so. Attempts have been made to get around the problems of Church and order, sometimes even with a curt dismissal of all such matters as irrelevant and unimportant. Very often it is said that a concern for and an interest in these matters is the sign of a petty ecclesiastical mind, intent upon insignificant traditional detail rather than upon the great and central matters of the faith. In this connection a cynic might remark that it is interesting to notice that the same sort of mind which now dismisses all questions of order as entirely unimportant is the one which twenty or thirty years ago regarded such theological doctrines as the Incarnation and the Trinitarian formula as nothing but a complication of the problem of Christian reunion, when all that was needed was agreement upon such "central matters" as God's Fatherhood, man's brotherhood, and Jesus' leadership.

The failure to recognize the serious nature of questions about the Church and the ministry, and an unwillingness to deal with these questions faithfully, is a very grave lapse from that intellectual integrity which has been traditional in historic Christianity of every sort. It may be that this lapse is to be put down to a prevalent confusion in modern thought, in which divine urgency and human haste are regarded as synonymous. It is, indeed, likely that if questions of Church and ministry could be put to one side, the reunion of the separated Christian bodies would be accomplished speedily enough. But in the long run, it is also likely that the kind of Christian reunion which would be achieved by such an evasion of, or by ambiguity about, these fundamental issues, the nature of the Church, the significance of its integral "structures," and the relation between the Church and these "structures," would be a reunion that was hardly worth the slight effort that would be required to obtain it. For the reunion of Christendom achieved on such a basis would be much more like a "gluing-together" of quite different entities than it would be the bringing into a genuine visible organic union, empirically known and externally expressed, of the several Christian bodies which at present are separated one from another.

The Nature of Reunion

If such a "gluing-together" is the end in view—and sometimes it has seemed that this was indeed the goal of certain advocates of reunion schemes—then it is necessary to say that Catholic-minded Christians of all kinds, and many others who would disown the name "catholic," are not interested. Ecumenicity, simply conceived on a federal level and thought of primarily as union in common work towards common ends, can be had through World Councils, National Councils, and the like. A reunited Church, without major commitments, could be achieved through simple agreement on the lowest common denominator of belief and practice. But if genuine empirical catholicity, which involves a true unity of all believers in the Body of Christ, is desired, there is only one way to achieve it. That is by a profound interest in, and by a genuine recovery of, the Church's historical tradition regarding the nature of the divine society and its ministering order. In a deep sense, the way forward is the way of return. Christianity is an historical, and an historically developed, religion, and the way to real reunion is not by devices for securing union on a level that disregards the past from which the future must grow.

It is, then, always better to speak honestly, although always in love, about these matters of belief and of practice which do in fact separate the Christian communions. To attempt to reach agreement by ambiguity, or through silence concerning the things which mean most to any of us, is bound to result in superficiality of approach and an unworthy conclusion. After all, the most important elements in any religion are usually not those which are held "in common" with other religions, but those wherein there may

be marked differences between the various groups. The
same principle holds true in the Christian world. Each
tradition, we may well believe, has in trust important truths
about our common heritage which must find their proper
place in the empirical unity after which we strive.

Thus we may say that the way towards a unity of Christians which will be according to the mind of Christ involves the frank sharing of our differences and the willingness to learn from these differences, as well as the finding
of agreement in common concerns. The only reunion which
is worth the effort that must necessarily be made in order to
accomplish it, will be a reunion that is based firmly on
principle and not upon simple expediency. It will be a
reunion which includes without diminution or loss the
fundamental truths which the several Christian traditions
believe that they have received as gifts from God, truths
for which therefore they must reverently and humbly contend. A shortcut which evades the discussion of these
points or which seeks by some ambiguous formula to smooth
over such profound differences will be found in the long
run to have disastrous consequences for the cause that all
Christians have at heart.

Leaders in the movement towards Christian reunion
have been learning this in recent years. This is the explanation of the "slowing-down" both in reunion discussions
and in the accomplishment of specific reunion schemes.
It is not that the spirit of the participants is any less earnest
and eager, nor that the desire for reunion is weakening.

Rather, it is that those who have been privileged to take part in such discussions and assist in the preparation of reunion plans have come to see that fundamentals are fundamental. If we hope to build well, we must dig deep. We have at last come to see that it is better to "make haste slowly" than to proceed at an almost reckless speed and run the risk of serious accident.

Furthermore the contemporary trend in theology—first on the continent of Europe, then in England, and now in America—has also had its part in this "slowing-down." No longer does the "reductionist" school of theology, usually known by the misnomer "liberal," have much influence in ecumenical circles. Theologians on every side and from every Christian tradition are seeking to enter more seriously and reverently into the given faith of the Church as this has come down to us through the centuries. The great thinkers of the Church's past are once again being heard with respect; in Mr. Chesterton's delightful phrase, we are ready once more "to give our ancestors a vote." This contemporary movement has led to an increasing conservatism in theological discussions. Sometimes, indeed, this is a reactionary conservatism; but more often it is a genuine willingness to learn from the past and a real unwillingness to throw over central emphases in that past in the interests of sheer contemporaneity. The cult of the contemporaneous which was so prevalent among us during the past half-century, has been succeeded by a new respect for Christian history and the lessons which it may teach us in our generation. So much is this the case that many of us feel obliged to reassert the "liberal" values so that all balance will not be lost.

Reunion and the Christian Tradition

In the light of this movement in theology, those who are interested in reunion are now forced to take account of the Church's developed and developing tradition. In doing this, they are forced also to take account of the given traditional ministry of the Church, which up until the continental Reformation was taken for granted everywhere in Christendom and is still taken for granted by the vast majority of Christian believers throughout the world. We are not called upon to "absolutize" that ministry, any more than we are called to follow ultra-montanist Roman Catholics and non-Roman "neo-Catholic" reactionaries in their attempt to "absolutize" the empirical Church itself. But we are called upon to "reverence and esteem" this ministry.

Anglicans especially have an obligation to argue, with certain of the Caroline divines in the Church of England, that while the traditional ministry does not "make" the Church, it is yet part of "the perfection of the Church." It would be profoundly unchristian to "unchurch" those bodies which through historical accident do not at this moment possess this ministry. But there is every reason for us to seek to commend it as the way to the fullest and most genuine "churching" of all Christians everywhere, and to do all in our power to make possible the widest sharing in this ministry.

No one in his senses would wish to make all those who do not already hold to the traditional episcopal ministry, based upon the ministerial priesthood of the Church, into "Episcopalians" in the denominational sense of the term. It is obvious that there are denominations and national churches, like the Church of Sweden, which hold the episcopal ministry, even if "as not holding it," for they do not always give it very strong emphasis, which are not in any denominational sense "Episcopalian." But if our argument in this book has any weight, it leads us to see how desirable it is that all existing ministries be given the fullest possible authentication, such as the episcopate historically and theologically offers. Above all, it leads us to the conviction that acceptance of the doctrine of ministerial priesthood, when rightly understood, is one way towards full catholicity, and especially towards that full apprehension of the Eucharist as the central, expressive Christian action of priestly worship, after which we must strive if we wish to be true to the witness of the ages and the apostolic nature of the Church's life.

Reunion and the Doctrine of Priesthood

We have pointed out that acceptance of the conception of the priestly character of the Church's ministry need not lead to false and unchristian notions. The approach to this priestly character taken by Dr. Moberly, which we have outlined in the next to the last chapter, shows that "the authority to offer the eucharistic sacrifice," to quote from Dr. Charles Gore's *The Church and the Ministry* (p. 182), "does not admit of being isolated from the other [pastoral] functions of the ministry," and that it may be held "as substantially constituting priesthood . . . without moral or intellectual disaster. The Christian priest is the Christian pastor." Even those who are fearful of the evils which in the later Roman Church have been associated with the notion of priesthood, must agree with Dr. William Sanday, when he wrote concerning Moberly's conception,

When the doctrine of a 'sacrificing priesthood' is presented in this way, I confess that I do not see why any of us should quarrel with it. I do not think that we do quarrel with it. If that sainted bishop [Lightfoot, whose volume *The Christian Ministry* was concerned to argue against unchristian sacerdotalism] . . . who brought out the stores of his learning to combat what is commonly known as 'sacerdotalism' could arise and be questioned, and have the theory of 'ministerial priesthood' set before him, I fully believe that he would not condemn but welcome it.[1]

So when Anglicans ask for acceptance of the practice of ordination by a bishop who is himself consecrated in an historical line of descent, it is not in the interests of a narrowing of Christianity. It is owing to the fact that Anglicans who so insist earnestly wish to share with others "who profess and call themselves Christian" the particular and precious heritage which they believe that the Anglican Communion, in common with other "Catholic" communions, has received as a gift from God through the Church of Christ. This means that they wish to share what they would call "the gift of holy order" in a sense which involves priestly function for the ministry.

Whether others may desire to share in this kind of ministerial authentication will depend, of course, upon whether they believe that Christianity is essentially that for which we have here argued: a religion which is itself priestly, with its central act of worship a priestly rite. We have sought in these chapters to interpret this conception in line with the New Testament and primitive Catholic teaching, to demonstrate that it involves no evil "sacerdotalism," no superstitious "priestcraft," no semi-magical "ritualism," no merely external "ceremonialism." If our statement of the case has any cogency, there should be no fundamental difficulty on the part of those whom Anglicans call "our separated brethren" in accepting the view of Christianity which requires, as its corollary, a priestly ministry functioning in and for the Church and for the Lord of the Church. Neither should there be any insurmountable obstacle to the acceptance of the episcopate as the symbol and steward of the priestly and apostolic faith, worship, and en-graced life.

It is impossible, however, to have any of these things without some theory of the ministry. Some doctrinal reason must be given. But the theory which is involved need not be the "Anglo-Catholic" view in its narrowest sense, for which, indeed, there is no real Anglican basis and which, *as often presented,* is neither scriptural nor catholic. What is required in accepting these things is simply that Christ, in and through His Spirit, and by and in His Church, carries on through the ministry His work of man's salvation, using towards this end the faithful proclamation of the Word, the right administration of the sacraments, and the continual empowering of His members through the Holy Spirit dwelling in His Body. This is the real meaning of the ministerial priesthood, effectually continued through the sacramental agency of the historical episcopate.

VIII

THE REUNION OF CHRISTENDOM

IF WHAT has been said in the preceding discussion comes
near the mark, we may be sure that the most hopeful and
promising sign for reunion today is not so much the prolonged discussions which have taken place between theologians of different denominations, important as these are,
but the constantly increasing emphasis which is being laid
everywhere through the Christian world on the centrality
of eucharistic worship and the growing awareness of the
fact that the Christian Church realizes and expresses its
own nature, in a unique fashion, in this act of worship.
While this emphasis is today found chiefly at the "top"
of the Protestant communions rather than widely spread
through the generality of congregations and parishes, it
is already making its impact felt at these "grass-roots" levels
and promises much for the future. An astounding number
of books has been published on this subject in recent years.
What is particularly significant is that these books are often
from inside communions whose eucharistic practice has
been very slight. One book, however, written in this instance by a member of the Disciples of Christ, who have

regular weekly communion services, sums up much contemporary American thought on the subject: Harold Fey's recent interesting study *The Lord's Supper: Seven Meanings.*

The Revival of Eucharistic Thought

In Great Britain, the revival of eucharistic thought among Free Churchmen is most marked. C. Harold Dodd has described the Eucharist in these words:

Here Christ is set before us incarnate, crucified, risen, and we partake of the benefits of his finished work, as contemporaries with it. We are neither merely recalling a story out of the past, nor merely expressing and nourishing a hope for the future, but experiencing in one significant rite the reality of the coming of Christ[1]

Dr. Nathaniel Micklem, formerly principal of Mansfield College in Oxford, has remarked in the course of his treatment of Christianity in the work entitled *Religion:*

The central act of Christian worship is the drama of the Mass or Communion Service, which is a memorial of the Passion of Christ, a eucharistic act of worship, an eschatological meal looking forward to the perfected Kingdom of God beyond this world.[2]

And Dr. Micklem states that, for Christian belief, "those who worthily partake of the holy meal do really partake of the life of Christ and are made one with him in the sacrament" (*op. cit.*, p. 188).

These and other English scholars, as well as continental theologians like Karl Barth, whose Gifford lectures on *The*

Knowledge of God and the Service of God exalted the place of the Lord's Supper in the Church's life, have had their influence upon American Protestant writers. The Anglican and Roman Catholic liturgical movements have also made their impact. The popular American editorial writer, Dr. Harold Fey, of the staff of *The Christian Century,* in his volume just mentioned, insists that the sacrament is central to the Christian life, since it is "the principal act of worship of the Christian faith" (*op. cit.,* page 16). Dr. Fey points out that there are many different aspects of the Eucharist: it is an act of remembrance, a thanksgiving, a covenant between God and man established by and in Jesus, "an affirmation and a renewal of the fellowship of the believer with Christ and with His Church," a feeding of the believer with "spiritual food," "a representation of the atonement," and a celebration and declaration of our Christian hope of immortality. Different bodies of Christians, Dr. Fey shows, have emphasized the different aspects; but if all these meanings may be found in this rite, it is obvious that it has an importance in Christianity which it is impossible to exaggerate.

The Significance of This Revival

The reason that we regard this movement in Protestant Christianity as so significant should be apparent from our whole line of reasoning. There is no likelihood of understanding the "Catholic" insistence on the priestly nature of the Church's life, the central action if its worship as a sacrifice of praise and thanksgiving, and the consequent necessity of a view of the ministry which is priestly in character, unless the Eucharist is taken to be the supremely characteristic action of the Body of Christ. When the Lord's Supper is, in practice, nothing more than a vestigial survival or, at the best, a very occasional and almost incidental event in the regular devotional life of the communicant, it is obvious that such considerations as those which we have adduced in this book will make no sufficient impact. No matter how much the Eucharist may be reverenced in theory, it will not have its full implication in the life of the communicant and his parish, nor will its wider meaning and its consequences in regard to Church and ministry be felt, unless it is in actual fact the centrally important service of Christian worship in weekly experience.

Readiness to see that the Lord's Supper is in sober truth the heart of the life of the Christian fellowship will lead those who by background and conviction are on the "Protestant" side of the Christian tradition to an appreciation of a ministry which functions sacramentally for the Church. They will be able to enter sympathetically into the conviction of "Catholic" Christians as to the meaning of the eucharistic action; and from this to see what is involved for such Christian brethren in their theory of the ministry. This, in turn, is certain to bring about a more sympathetic attitude towards the idea of the traditional Christian ministry and the "Catholic" concern for an ordaining organ of the Church which can act as "steward for the mysteries of Christ," and thus give an authentication to the ordained ministry such as shall leave no shadow of doubt that the offering of the "continual remembrance" is according to our Saviour's command and in the intention of fulfilling His purpose.

The Importance of Preaching the Word

But there is something to be said on the other hand. It is imperative that the "Catholic" Christian recognize that the "Protestant" emphasis upon the preaching of the Word holds a place, and an indispensable and rightful place, in the Christian tradition. The preaching of the Word must necessarily be associated with, although it is not identical with, the "administration of the sacraments." In scriptural and early Christianity the two go together. The sacraments, and especially the Eucharist as the expressive action of the Body of Christ, are seen along with the preaching of the Word, which marks out and gives relevance to the sacramental reality of participation in Christ. The minister of Christ's Church is to be faithful in the preaching of the Gospel as well as in the administration of the sacraments. There can be no doubt that the stress on the Word, whose recovery has been the glory of evangelical Christianity, has not been found so fully in the "Catholic" communions. But both are necessary.

There Are Differences in Ministries

Protestant denominations cannot assert that their ministries, in actual practice, are exactly the same as those of the "Catholic communions," when at the same time many in these denominations are clear that they have come into existence precisely as a protest against the whole notion of a priesthood attaching to the ministry. These denominations are now being led to see that there are genuine values, and indeed necessary elements, in the ancient tradition of a ministerial and sacrificing priesthood. Abuse and superstition so overlaid these values that in the days of the Reformation it was necessary to make violent protest. But in our present situation they should be equally ready to welcome whatever action or commission will give to their ministry the priestly character which it has lost through the vicissitudes of an earlier historical situation.

It is indeed true that the "Catholic" communions have maintained this priestly authentication through the ordination of their ministry by an apostolic instrument claiming continuity with the Church's apostolic days. But this does not constitute any adequate reason why "Catholic" communions should be unwilling to make their own concessions. Technically speaking, there may be nothing "defective" in the priestly character of the Catholic ministries. But there is certainly no doubt that in practice they have been and still are lacking in that emphasis on the Word which Protestantism stresses. Hence, while Catholics can hardly say that a "prophet" is ordained when in fact he is "recognized" for what he is, they ought to be ready to welcome whatever act of authorization for *the preaching of the Word of God* their separated brethren might ask, in virtue of which their gift of ministering may be enhanced and they may receive such additional grace and power as the commissioning of ministers in Protestant denomina-

tions conveys. To them, too, it might thus be made clear
that the duty and the privilege of "preaching the Word
of God" has been given, in the fullest sense of the phrase
—and in a sense which the "Protestant" communions
would recognize and accept.

It is difficult to see why such a gesture on the part of
"Catholic" Christians is sometimes regarded with horror by
some Churchmen. The reality of the Catholic ministries
would in no sense be denied, so far as any sound scriptural
and patristic theology of order can see. What would happen would be the addition of such specific authorization as
would satisfy those who feel that an entirely one-sided con-
cession by "Protestants" would be equivalent to denying all
the efficacy in, and the obvious divine blessing of, non-
episcopalian ministries. On the other hand, the frank ad-
mission that something can be received by the "Catholic"
ministry from the "Protestant" traditions would make it possible for the "Protestant" ministry, with better grace and
more readiness of heart and acquiescence in mind, to receive the kind of authentication which is implied in Catholic order.

Constant harping by some "Catholics" on questions of
"validity" has only confused the whole issue. We have seen
that "validity" is a purely technical term; and in any event,
the sort of procedure we are suggesting does not in any way
imperil whatever significance the concept may possess in
the present broken state of Christendom. Without attempting an uncharitable judgment, we must say that the
refusal of intransigent "Catholics" to support the Church

of South India—which safeguards the essentials of the Catholic tradition while it also finds place for the values of the Protestant ministries—is very difficult to understand. It seems much like "biting off one's nose to spite one's face."

Some Heartening Developments

It is not our purpose to enter into any detailed discussion of present-day schemes for Christian reunion. But it must be said that certain of these recent proposals—in Australia, North India, and Ceylon—appear entirely adequate in the light of the considerations which we have offered; while the Church of South India is entirely in accord with them. Of course, what needs to be safeguarded is the integrity of each tradition, in order as well as in faith. The one regrettable detail of the South India plan seems to be the loss of an important aspect of the historic episcopate: its place as final steward of the faith, under God in Christ, is endangered by the possibility of rejection of its actions by the other orders of the Church's assembly. Would it not be more in accord with the traditional function of the bishops to allow the other orders' right to delay, question, revise, but not to *veto*, the decisions of the collective episcopate? But it is lamentable that attacks on the Church of South India have failed to see the enormous value of that experiment, by concentrating upon some few insignificant details that are not integral to the Church's life. It surely does not appear, even to some moderately critical observers, that the Catholic side was, as it is often said, "sold down the river." [3] In any event it seems that it would certainly be wiser and more charitable to adopt a policy of watchful *and helpful* cooperation rather than giving the whole program an outright and total condemnation. It is along such lines that we shall make most progress.

Eastern and Roman Views

It would be preposterous to discuss reunion questions without some attention to the Eastern Orthodox communion and the Roman Church. In regard to the Orthodox groups, it is safe to say that it is not at all impossible to envisage real steps towards eventual reunion, once the historical circumstances permit. The Orthodox approach to the fundamental question of faith and order in relationship to the Church as the living Body of Christ is very similar to that which we have put forward. Indeed, the line of argument here presented is so much in line with that taken by many Orthodox theologians in their discussion of reunion that the writer has often found his most cordial support at ecumenical gatherings from those of Orthodox persuasion. The Orthodox theory of "economy" will doubtless play its part in our discussions with the Orthodox, who would very likely be willing to assert that if the external steps necessary to what they consider right churchmanship were taken, the Church (by which they mean, of course, the Orthodox communions) could recognize these ministries. Unity in faith and in common life would make "validation" a real possibility. This would certainly be true so far as the Anglican ministries are concerned. There would be necessary accommodations required from "Protestant" Christians; but the principle of generous hospitality would still hold good, once assurances were given in regard to the total organism of Christian faith, worship, and life. The Anglican Communion occupies a very strategic place in this picture, for it can mediate between Orthodoxy and "Protestant" Christianity. This is one reason why Anglicans should be cautious about easy schemes for union with Protestant denominations which, unlike the Church of South India and the proposals in North India, Ceylon, and Australia, might endanger their position vis-à-vis Orthodoxy.

As to the Roman Church, little can be said with any certainty. What may be accomplished some day in bringing about closer relations with Rome, and how this may be done, is for the future to show. One thing, however, is perfectly plain. The Roman Church must have its place in any realistic appraisal of reunion possibilities. This is all too frequently forgotten by "Protestants" who seem sometimes to put the Roman Church so far outside their field of thought that it might just as well belong to the non-Christian world. It is, indeed, one of the most disquieting things about many reunion discussions and many conferences on ecumenical matters, that so often the implication is that only the "Protestant" groups, together with Anglicanism, Old Catholicism, and sometimes Eastern Orthodoxy, are taken into consideration as "the Christian Church." This surely is unrealistic and uncharitable; to put it more bluntly, it is unchristian nonsense.

Those of us who are not of the Roman obedience cannot

help feeling that recent theological developments in the Roman Church (e.g., the dogmatic definitions of the Immaculate Conception and the Bodily Assumption of St. Mary), and the place within the Roman Church that is given to the Pope of Rome, are the result of a lopsided and erroneous development in western Christianity. The claim to infallibility, as at present stated and maintained, is impossible of acceptance by any non-Roman Christian. This claim rests upon a whole set of assumptions, both as to the nature of the Church and the function of the Roman Patriarchate, which in our judgment is theologically fallacious, even though the development of papal authority may be historically explicable as the result of pressures which forced the growth of one ancient see to a pretentious, and almost demonic, pride of place and power.

But, at the same time, the papacy, in some sense and in some form, will certainly be an element in any realistic plan for the empirical expression of the whole Church's catholicity. Certainly, we do not see how the papacy can be fitted into a Christianity which is Catholic in the scriptural, primitive, and "rightly-developing" sense. But God may have ways which are beyond our present seeing, if only we will be patient and wait for His guidance, while we still continue both to maintain the Catholic "structures" of faith, worship, life, and ministry, and at the same time to welcome the Reformation recovery of the "evangel" which is at the heart of that Catholic truth. Roman Catholicism most certainly is not, as it falsely claims to be, the only genuine element in Christian tradition. But we must all agree that the Roman Church, despite what we regard as its faults, is integral to the Christian tradition as a whole. Reunion schemes which neglect to take account of the Roman Church, or which are constructed without recognition of its existence, are by that very token self-condemned; they are less than truly ecumenical and far less than truly Catholic.

A Concluding Observation

And now we have come to the end of our appointed task. It is hardly likely that either our approach or conclusions have pleased or satisfied everyone. But one thing we may hope. We have attempted to speak honestly, but charitably, of our differences. We have endeavoured to put the case for the traditional ministry and the priestly nature of that ministry with a due recognition of the difficulties that others have found in it; we have sought to show that the case for that ministry is bound up with the case for "Catholic" Christianity as a whole. But we have also attempted to argue that this does not mean that the communions, springing from Reformation days or later periods, are "beyond the pale," as some extremists assert. Rather we have said that the case for the Catholic view of the ministry can be put with a real appreciation and a hearty acceptance of the values to be found in the "Protestant" communions. We have defended the Church of South India and recent proposals elsewhere which offer a way, not of dismissing the present differences in spirit and atmosphere between the "Catholic" and the "Protestant" apprehensions of Christianity, but of establishing a rich unity in which these different emphases are included and transcended. So we hope that, through God's Spirit and by the charity of men which is His gift, we may grow together, slowly perhaps but very surely. One can only pray that God will bless this and every other attempt to speak, in love and sympathy, what seems the truth, to the end that His Son's prayer may be answered: *that they all may be one; as thou, Father, art in me, and I in thee, that they also may be one in us: that the world may believe that thou hast sent me.*

AUTHOR'S NOTES

CHAPTER I

1. This position is hinted in many places in the course of the contributions to the monumental symposium *The Apostolic Ministry* and is explicitly stated in that volume in a quotation made from William Bright by the editor, the late Bishop of Oxford. This error is the suggestion that somehow the clergy "make" the Church. "If we have to choose," writes Dr. Kirk (*Apostolic Ministry*, p. 26), "between a doctrine which makes the ministry wholly dependent upon the Chuch, and one which endows it with independence from everything except its original divine commission, the latter is the one which we must embrace." Dr. Kirk admits that this is an unnatural and unnecessary dilemma. But he insists that if the dilemma were forced, he with his fellow-writers would be "obliged to assign independence and therefore priority to the ministry." Here he quotes Bright's extraordinary statement: "The Church began in a clergy" (p. 30). See also the admirable critique of *The Apostolic Ministry* in *The Historic Episcopate in the Fullness of the Church* (ed. by K. M. Carey).

2. This view is suggested in Dr. Theodore O. Wedel's otherwise valuable and illuminating study, *The Coming Great*

Church. Canon Wedel sees that priesthood must be grounded first and essentially in the being of the Body of Christ itself. But he does not appear to recognize so clearly—or at least he does not state the view with any clarity—that this truth, present as it must be in the inner life of the Church, can really have no permanent significance for men living historical lives, unless it is visibly and externally expressed and made manifest (compare *op. cit.,* Chapter IV, passim).

3. In Dr. Dodd's book *History and the Gospel* we are told (p. 138) that fellowship in the Church "is the historical embodiment of the Kingdom of God as the gift of eternal life"; while in his treatment of the relation of Scripture and the Church in *The Bible Today* he puts it in even stronger terms than this. Another Cambridge Free Church theologian, Dr. R. Newton Flew, carries on this same line of thought in *Jesus and His Church.* In the United States, Dr. John Knox has asserted that we are "dependent upon the Church," both for our knowledge of the gospel and for our appropriation of it. He speaks of the Church as "the continuation of the event" which is the coming of God in Christ through His mighty act of incarnation (*The Meaning of Christ,* p. 97), and in his recent Hoover lectures, *The Early Church and the Coming Great Church,* Dr. Knox argues for the necessity of the Church as an immediate corollary of the Christ-event—essentially the view maintained here.

4. Mersch, in his *Morality and the Mystical Body,* writes of the Church as "that organism . . . in which Christ continues to be attached to his own" (p. 55). His discussion shows a complete break with legalism, and a strong emphasis on the "integral humanism," as he calls it, which marks the Church's life in Christ.

Karl Adam, whose book *The Spirit of Catholicism* is one of the most attractive works defending the position of his communion, defines the Church as a divine creation with an "organic unity" (*op. cit.*, p. 32). Doctrine, worship, moral life, piety, even the hierarchical structural of the Church itself, are all seen by Adam as functions in this organic unity. Dr. Adam explicitly tells us that this unity is "no mere mechanical unity, but a unity with an inner differentiation," which is his way of defining a unity that is deeply organic rather than merely organizational in nature (*loc. cit.*).

5. In his essay in the symposium, *The Apostolic Ministry* (which is the one essay in that work that can be commended almost without qualification), Father Hebert continues this same thought as it applies to the ministerial functioning of the Church, understood always as the living Body of the Living Lord. The writer may also be permitted to refer here to his own book *His Body the Church*, where the attempt was made to gather up the new Catholic thinking, which is indeed the old thinking, about the Church and to re-state the doctrine of the Body of Christ in terms governed by a vitalistic and organic view of the meaning of Christian fellowship.

6. A work such as Dr. Sergei Boulgakoff's *The Orthodox Church* and essays such as those lately appearing in ecumenical journals from the pen of Dr. Georges Florowsky, former Dean of St. Vladimir's Seminary in New York and now professor at Harvard Divinity School, have made this Eastern position clear to the rest of the Christian world.

7. Dr. Dillistone's views have more recently been modified; and his statements on the subject in *The Structure of the Divine Society* are very close to those expressed in this book. In his earlier work, Dr. Dillistone had criticized the views of the writer, as well as those of L. S. Thornton and others, because they seemed to him to go "beyond the strict evidence of the new Testament" (*op. cit.*, p. 60). He felt that emphasis

on biological language, and deductions from it, are at best "legitimate as commentary, suggestion, and illustration" (*loc. cit.*).

8. In *The Ministry of the Church*, p. 28. If Bishop Neill means, however, that it is unchristian to make the ministry, *tactually conveyed*, the "essence" of the meaning of the Church, we must of course agree with him, as the last few pages indicate.

CHAPTER II

1. This position is miles apart from the kind of Christian thinking which would confine our religion to its swaddling clothes or to its perambulator. Unquestionably our view approaches, in certain respects, the view taken by some of the Roman Catholic "modernists" in the early decades of this century. But it is not the extreme view which the Roman Curia rightly condemned in these men, if indeed they taught the ideas attributed to them. At least some of the Roman "modernists" appear to have been altogether indifferent to history. Some of them thought, for example, that the Christ of faith could still be worshipped even if the Jesus of history were so vaguely known that he might just as well never have lived in Palestine. Some, even more extremely, may have held that the Jesus of Nazareth was indeed irrelevant to the faith of the Church in the living Christ. If this was the position of some Roman "modernists," then it does indeed make nonsense of Christianity and completely destroy the peculiar *differentia* of our faith.

CHAPTER III

1. We have sought here to provide only the material which seems directly relevant to our present purpose. For a full discussion, reference may be made to more detailed historical analyses, especially those of Dr. Burn-Murdoch (*Church Continuity and Unity*), and the symposium, *The Historic Episcopate in the Fullness of the Church.* These writers support with adequate evidence our contention that it is entirely reasonable to say that the development of the Christian ministry to its regular form of bishop-priest-deacon is, indeed, "in a straight line" and represents no fundamental nor significant deviation from what the New Testament shows us of "the mind of Christ" and of primitive practice.

CHAPTER V

1. Moberly, *Ministerial Priesthood,* pp. 254-55. All quotations from this work are made by permission of the publisher.

2. The *Report of the Commission on Doctrine in the Church of England,* is quoted by permission of the publisher.

CHAPTER VI

1. William Temple, *The Church Looks Forward,* pp. 24-25. Quoted by permission of the publisher.

2. *The Historic Episcopate in the Fullness of the Church.*

Author's Notes

CHAPTER VII

1. Sanday, *Conception of the Priesthood,* p. 92. Quoted by permission of the publisher.

CHAPTER VIII

1. Dodd, *History and the Gospel,* pp. 163-64. Quoted by permission of the publisher.

2. Micklem, *Religion,* p. 188. Quoted by permission of the publisher.

3. *Cf.* A. E. J. Rawlinson's *Problems of Reunion* and *The Church of South India* for an admirable defence of this experiment, a defence with which this writer would entirely agree.

BIBLIOGRAPHY

Anglican Orders: Being the Answer of the Archbishops of England to the Bull of His Holiness, Pope Leo XIII.

London: S.P.C.K., 1943.

Report of the Commission on Doctrine in the Church of England.

London: S.P.C.K., 1938.

Adam, Karl. *The Spirit of Catholicism.*

London: Sheed and Ward, 1939.

Barth, Karl. *The Knowledge of God and the Service of God.*

London: Hodder & Stoughton, 1928.

Boulgakoff, Sergei. *The Orthodox Church.*

London: Centenary Press, 1935.

Burn-Murdoch, H. *Church Continuity and Unity.*

Cambridge: Cambridge University Press, 1945.

Carey, K. M., ed. *The Historic Episcopate in the Fullness of the Church.*

London: Dacre Press, 1954.

Dillistone, F. W. *The Word of God and the People of God.*

London: Church Book Room Press, 1948.

——. *The Structure of the Divine Society.*

Philadelphia: Westminster Press, 1951.

Dodd, C. Harold. *The Bible Today.*

Cambridge: Cambridge University Press, 1947.

——. *History and the Gospel.*

London: Nisbet, 1938.

Ehrhardt, Arnold. *The Apostolic Succession in the First Two Centuries of the Church.*
London: Lutterworth Press, 1953.

Fey, Harold. *The Lord's Supper: Seven Meanings.*
New York: Harper & Brothers, 1948.

Flew, R. Newton. *Jesus and His Church.*
Nashville: Abingdon Press, 1938.

Gore, Charles. *The Church and the Ministry.*
London: S.P.C.K., revised edition, 1936.

Grant, Frederick C. *Introduction to New Testament Thought.*
Nashville: Abingdon Press, 1950.

Hebert, A. G. *The Form of the Church.*
London: Faber and Faber, 1944.

Kirk, Kenneth E., ed. *The Apostolic Ministry.*
London: Hodder & Stoughton, 1946.

Knox, John. *The Early Church and the Coming Great Church.*
Nashville: Abingdon Press, 1955.

———. *The Meaning of Christ.*
New York: Charles Scribner's Sons, 1947.

Mascall, E. L. *Theology* (June 1949).

Mersch, Emile. *La Théologie du Corps Mystique.*
Paris: Desclée de Brouwer, 1949.

Micklem, Nathaniel. *Religion.*
Oxford: Oxford University Press, 1948.

Moberly, R. C. *Ministerial Priesthood.*
London: John Murray, 1910.

Neill, Stephen, ed. *The Ministry of the Church.*
London: Canterbury Press, 1947.

Nock, A. D. *Conversion.*
London: Oxford University Press, 1933.

Pittenger, W. N. *His Body the Church.*
New York: Morehouse-Gorham, 1945.

Biblilography

Rawlinson, A. E. J. *Problems of Reunion.*
    London: Eyre and Spottiswoode, 1950.
    ————. *The Church of South India.*
    London: Hodder & Stoughton, 1951.
Robinson, William. *The Biblical Doctrine of the Church.*
    St. Louis: Bethany Press, 1948.
Sanday, William. *Conception of the Priesthood.*
    London: Longmans Green, 1899.
Streeter, B. H. *The Primitive Church.*
    London: Macmillan, 1929.
Temple, William. *The Church Looks Forward.*
    London: Macmillan, 1944.
Thomas Aquinas. *Summa Theologica.*
    St. Louis: Benziger Brothers, 1947.
Tyrrell, George. *Scylla and Charybdis.*
    London: Longmans Green, 1907.
Wedel, Theodore O. *The Coming Great Church.*
    New York: Macmillan Company, 1945.

224-257-C-3.5

DATE DUE

12/86			